ŞANGÓ

The Cult of Kingship

An Anthology
by

IYALOŞA AYOBUNMI SOSI ŞANGODÉ

ISBN:9781502719829

Dedication

This book is dedicated to My Master Teachers, Oluwo Edubi Ifamunyiwa Ajamu, Oluwo Medahochi Kofi Zannu, H.R.H. Oba Oseijeman A. O. Adefunmi I, and Renaud Sangodei Alafia Simmons.

"May They Rest In Perfect Peace"

A c k n o w l e d g m e n t s

My Most Grateful Thanks to the Late "OBA OSEIJEMAN A. ADEFUNMI I", His Royal Highness "Oba of Oyotunji African Village".
"Father of the African Cultural Restoration Movement in America", without You None of this would have been possible.

Also to my First Master Teacher and Husband "Oluwo Chief Edubi Ifamunyiwa Ajamu" who brought me into the Understanding of My African Ancestors and the Knowledge of "The GODS of AFRICA", and to my Godfather "HL Chief Medahochi Kofi Zannu" the First *"Araba Ifa"* of North America, without who's encouragement the "African American School of *Orisa/Vodun* Theology" and the "ADEFUNMI RITES of INITIATION" may never have been a reality.

"MAY THEY REST IN PERFECT PEACE"

Contents

Forward

Red lord of fire, third King of Oyo
calls us by the thunder!
His lightning burns all liars!
(A praise poem to SANGO)

The great value of Pagan religion over Christianity, Judaism, and Islam, is that 'the Pagan religions very carefully and scientifically define All human types.' This is not possible in the "One God" religions. This means that as religions they are Incomplete. They do not go far enough into the Depths of Human Life. They are "One Cult" religions. Thus they have failed to improve human kind. In fact through their mission, they have Destroyed many noble human virtues and characteristics. They kept the world in chaos.

The Ancient Religion of the "Yoruba" of Nigeria is one of those great Polytheistic, Multi-cult, Pagan systems. It has provided human society with the knowledge of the vast Pantheon of Gods and Goddesses which actually control human life and who are the causes of its miseries and success.

During the *"SANGO"* Festival we are presented with a case in point. An example of the classification of Divine Complexes which enable certain human types to find themselves in their God.

"SANGO" is a Divine Prototype, a God, a Divinity or an African Saint (whichever you prefer) to whom all of those born with certain fiery proclivities, certain bombastic temperaments, may identify.

Since such an extrovert Aquarian temperament could hardly find full expression in the introvert watery Piscean Cult of Jesus, it would find itself without a spiritual identity.

If forced into Christianity, it would be considered sinful and cursed. Yet, if nature produces such types, it must have an important role for them. It is the duty of a truly spiritual religion to find it, and to refine it when it becomes socially destructive.

This is why African religion has Fire Gods, Water Gods, Earth Gods, and Air Gods. It is why human types can "find" themselves: and by a study of the characteristics of their patron God or Goddess can understand more perfectly, the strange moods, events, failures and triumphs of their lives.

Now, because all of us have a little bit of *"SANGO"* in our nature, and we may be disposed to mildly suppress it or to strenuously control it, we take the time each year to release it and to celebrate it in a controlled period. We thus relieve ourselves of a psychological depression, or of a sense of total self denial.

Long Live The Worship of Fire! Long Live The Cult of *"SANGO"*!

HRH Oba Ofuntola Oseijeman A. Adefunmi I
King of the Yoruba of North America
Oyotunji Village, South Carolina

Religion
The Gods Of Africa
by
HRH Oba Ofuntola Oseijeman A. Adefunmi I

Religion is a Regional, Tribal and Nationalistic Philosophy. Each people in each region of the earth have one. The idea of one religion converting peoples of other nations, races, and regions is arrogant, imperialistic and unsuitable, because each religion is based upon geographical peculiarities, the customs and philosophies of a people and legends handed down to them by Their Ancestors. To covert one people then to the religion of another people is to interrupt the natural continuity of Self Knowledge, history and culture of a people. An example is the conversion of South American Indians, to Christianity; for such people to be told that the Jordan River, the city of Bethlehem, a sacrificial Jew, ancient Hebrew and Middle Eastern history and philosophies are sacred to them is mischievous and produces an Abnormal Psychosis. Because of respect for the cultures of all peoples, and the wisdom of all peoples to adapt intelligently to their environment, Africans have never commenced proselytizing their numerous religions.

The Africans, from time immemorial have respected Two Worlds. The Physical World and the Metaphysical World, or the Universe of visible and tangible forces, and the Universe of invisible and intangible forces. The entire psychology of African Civilizations is predicated on this knowledge. The African observes that the Physical World is governed by the Metaphysical World, in the same way that the behavior of a person is governed by his *Spiritual* nature. The African therefore is a student of Metaphysical Law, and those men and women *specializing* in this science are called Priests.

The European as the opposite, is a student of Physical Laws and people specializing in this study are called Scientists.

Naturally there are exceptions to this generalization, but it provides us with an insight as to why Europeans have reached such a spectacular Material civilization, while their Religion is a simple dichotomy in which the world is divided into Good or Evil. Certain things are ruled by a demonic evil God (Satan). With such a childlike concept, Europeans and peoples conquered by them and converted to their way of thinking have become extremely inhibited and confused, and a general Spiritual (called psychological by them) Sickness pervades their lives.

Among Africans, ever since the great days of Nubia, Kush, and Egypt, there has been an increasing trend towards the perfect Spiritual Civilization, and the development of Material aspects has been correspondingly neglected.

To the African, things cannot be classified as Good or Evil, right or wrong. All things are Relatively Negative or Positive depending upon the situation and the positions each person is in.

For example: to kill is not in itself wrong, it depends upon the situation one is in whether it is necessary or not. So it is with everything in life, all is relative.

There is no such nonsense as Sin, but there are Laws, thousands of them, which may be different for every person, place or thing.

But every natural or supernatural, person, place, thing or activity is subject each to its own laws, the Violation of which is the cause of calamity and unhappiness.

With so vast a concept, called superstition by Europeans but, which is ever present in the minds of Africans, it is obvious why the materialistic wonders of Nubia, Kush, Egypt, Ghana or Zimbabwe were not duplicated.

We may conclude that whereas Europeans were and are preoccupied with the perfection of Objects, the Africans were and are preoccupied with the perfection of the Human Being.

The Ancestors of the *Yoruba* originally inhabited Meroe and Upper Egypt, and their religion is fundamentally the same as that of the Ancient Nubians and Egyptians.

The Yoruba worship 401 Gods. The Supreme God is called the *"OLODUMARE"* or the *"OLORUN"* ("The Owner of Heaven") and is analyzed as a "Universal Energy" which permeates all things.

The *"OLORUN"* is not worshipped, it has no priests, nor chants, nor rituals and no personality nor sex. It is merely 'the first order of the universe', the Highest Cosmic Energy which being omnipresent may be taken for granted, because neither sacrifice nor prayer can Influence its inevitable and eternal inscrutability. Second to the *"OLORUN"* is a vast and intricate network or lesser *forces* and *energies* which more directly influence earthly life and its cycles. Such forces as sunlight, rain, electricity, sickness, vegetation, oceans, love, luck, etc.

These "Energies" or vibrations have character and temperament, and it is those that mankind may reasonably direct his petitions and sacrifices for mercy, relief, increase or protection.

The Ancient Yoruba *Personified* these forces and called them the *"ORISA"*, their neighbors the *Dahomians* call them the *"VODUN"*. Other peoples have called these secondary "Divine Forces", Saints, Gods, Angels, etc. The Ancient Kushites called them *"Zar"*, the Hebrews who derived most of their religious knowledge and practices from the Egyptians, called a group of them the *"Elohim"*.

Universally, the pattern seems to be to give these higher forces the names of great National Heroes who seemed during their lifetime to possess characteristics comparable to such forces. In other words they were an Earthly Manifestation of a GOD. For example, *"SANGO"* the turbulent 'Third King of the OYO Yoruba' (c.1400?) is identified with "Thunder and Lightning". Among Europeans, "Saint Barbara" is the same personification; in India it is the God "Indra", in China it is "San Kan Fong", in Hebrew mythology it is "Barakiel", in Ancient Egypt it was "Osiris".

The Yoruba, like their Nubian, Kushite and Egyptian forefathers, and like All peoples and races who produce sculptured or pictorial images of Spiritual Beings – are "Idolaters".

The Philosophy of Idolatry is that a "Visual Representation", of the ideal type an individual aspires to become, is an imperative aid in helping a person to identify himself with His GOD.

In the endless campaign of rituals performed before such images, the relationship between worshipper and whatever is worshipped becomes unshakably unified. Every human being and even every nation has its Ideal Type, and it is for this reason that the Idols of each People reflect Their Racial Characteristics. It is this which provides each race or people with its self-containment, belief in divine origin, their pride and genius.

It is interesting to observe that Africans born in America, those contemptuously called "Negroes" have had all European Idols and Ideals put in place of Their Own Idols, have lost all sense of the Natural Genius of the rest of the African Race and have frustrated generation after generation in a pitiful attempt to make themselves Look like the Europeans.

African Religion is essentially Polytheistic or Pagan. The word *Pagan* comes from the Latin "pagani", which means "country folk".

Yoruba religion is mainly the worship of the many *"Orisa"* included among which are some of the *"Vodun"* borrowed from the Dahomeans. We may call this religion *"Orisa/Vodun"*. The principle reason certain Africans do not emphasize the worship of the Supreme Deity (*"Olorun"*) is that it is believed man should be able to identify with and try to be like his God. Obviously no man could think of being like *"OLORUN"*, and to emphasize such a worship would destroy the intimate relationship between man and his God, which must be the end to which religion works. Upon this reasoning, 'each person worships a National or Racial personification of the Divine Energy to which his own nature corresponds.' This is his *"ORISA"*.

The method of discovering which "Orisa or Vodun" is incarnated in ones body is through Divination. The Yoruba and Fon have a special "Priesthood" of master diviners called "Babalawo". Though these men are called 'witch doctors' by Europeans and Arabs, they are Africa's Medium of Correspondence with The Forces which govern life.

Though Islam and Christianity both have brought a conflict of theology since their introduction into Africa, it is astounding to what degree African Religion, without a holy book nor a prophet nor missionaries, has been able to Withstand their combined attacks, and shows signs of a Great New Resurgence.

West African "Yoruba" Religion is often regarded as the "roots" of the most Widespread African Religion in the World. The Religion of the "OYO" sub-group of the Yoruba has been the most Fundamental Single Influence on the Brazilian "Condomble" and "Xango" Religions, on the Cuban of "Santeria" and on the Trinidadian "Sango" Religion.

While the 19th century Slave Trade planted the "Yoruba Gods", or *"ORISA"*, on Latin American soil, 20th century Nationalism fertilized their spread, and migration transplanted them to virtually every City on the American Continent.

Government
The Sacred State

The government of the "Yoruba", like that of certain other Ancient West African peoples is based upon a principle of correspondence with "Nature", in this instance, the "Heavenly Bodies". Since Long Ago, Africans discovered the secrets of Astronomy and Astrology and the essential Influence which the arrangement and cycles of these Forces play in the government of the cosmos. They have, from Prehistoric Times, patterned the positions and offices of their own earthly government after the example of The Heavens. Concluding that since Earth is ruled by the Heavens, the people of Earth can do no better than imitate that eternal and perfect pattern in governing themselves. "Ohene ye Owia", "The King is the Sun", is an "Ashanti" proverb. The "Queen-mothers" of African states correspond to the "Moon". The Queen-mother is conceived as the 'Owner of the State', and The "King" is the 'Ruler of the State'. Incidentally, this indicates the High position which Women play in politics.

This concept permits the Secretary of State, "Bashorun", to correspond to Mercury; the War department to Mars; the Health department to Saturn; the Social Welfare departments to Jupiter; Cultural departments to Venus; Special Scientific departments to Neptune and so on. Among the "Yoruba Gods" these planets more or less correspond to *"Obatala"* (Sun), *"Yemoja"* (Moon), *"Esu"* (Mercury), *"Ogun"* (Mars), *"Babaluaiye"* (Saturn), *"Osun"* (Venus), *"Olokun"* (Neptune), and so on.

It is for this reason that the Heads of these departments are considered "Sacred" and therefore that 'the State is Sacred', with The King as the "High-Priest" of The Nation.

It is interesting how many Ancient and intellectual peoples used this same principle in the organization of their long, stable governments: the "Aztecs" and "Incas", the "Hindu", the "Javanese", "Japanese", "Chinese", "Ancient Egyptians", "Greeks" and "Romans", to name but a few.

The King of the "OYO-Yoruba" is called the "ALAAFIN", which means "Owner of the Palace". At the time of the Zenith of The Empire, there were 1060 Provincial Kings. The title "OBA" (King) is given to

Heads of states, towns, villages and certain societies. This greatly confused the uninformed Europeans who thought that Africa was divided into as many separate nations as there were Kings. These "Kings" rather corresponded to the different orders of the English Peerage (Dukes, Viscounts, Barons, etc.), and each one knows his place. The "Onikoyi" as Head of the Metropolitan Province used to head them all to "OYO" once a year to pay homage to the "ALAAFIN".

The "Alaafin" is a direct descendant of King *"ODUDUA"*, the Founder of the Nation, who it is said was one of the Last Kings of *"Meroe"*, the great NUBIAN state. The office is Hereditary in the same family, But not necessarily from father to son. The "Alaafin" is elected from among many eligible members of the Royal Family by a Powerful Society of Yoruba Noblemen know as the "Oyo Mesi", the seven principal councilors of state. There have been 43 "Alaafin", all drawn from the Same Dynasty which has ruled The Yoruba for over 2,000 years.

Before he is crowned "OBA", The "Alaafin-elect" must become a *PRIEST*, usually a Priest of *"SANGO"*, the Deified "FOURTH KING of The

YORUBA", and "THIRD ALAAFIN of OYO", who is worshipped as "The THUNDERGOD".

The "Alaafin" has as much *Spiritual* as well as purely Political work to perform being at once "King" and "Priest" of the State.

For three months before Coronation, the "Alaafin-elect" remains strictly in private learning and practicing the style and deportment of a Monarch, and the details and functions of his office. During this period he is dressed in black and is entitled to use a "cap of state", called *"Ori-ko-gbe-ofo"* ("head may not remain uncovered"). The affairs of state at this time are conducted by the "Bashorun", Secretary of the State.

The Palace or "The Alafin", is an enormous structure covering a vast area. It is in itself a walled Village in which lives the huge Palace population composed of wives, ilari, noblemen, eunuchs, messengers, guards, slaves, the Kings horses, etc. The highest ranking Female in the Palace is "Iya-Oba" who is the Kings official "Mother", his own mother having been asked to "go to sleep", i.e., take poison and die (go into exile), so that the King need never Humble himself before Anyone, because should he do so, as 'The Symbol of The Nation', it would be a sign of

National Humility. Conclusively, the position of Women in politics has been Extremely Powerful.

Though the Kings terms of office is Constitutionally for Life, although, he may be Voted Out of office should he 'Embarrass the Nation' or lose the confidence of the people or high statesmen. He must die that very day by taking poison before sundown; he is then buried honorably in the "*BARA*", the Mausoleum of Deceased Kings.

The Blood Kin of Royalty naturally posed a Special Threat to any reigning King: they were qualified to usurp the throne. Throughout "OYO's" Royal History and politics, was the Palace's mistrust of the Royal Family. In order to deter parricide, the "Aremo" (Crown Prince) was killed upon the King's death, until "Alaafin, ATIBA" ended this policy in 1858. However, even "Alaafin, Atiba" kept the princes away from the palace.

The Kings Royal Kinsmen were also excluded from appointments as Commanders of the "OYO" Capital's Army, lest they take the Crown through Martial Force.

Outsiders without any claim by Birth to the Throne, the "AYABA" (wives of the reigning King, and his predecessors), were Entrusted somewhat more safely with administrative functions, rights and privileges. They served as Heads of Empire-wide "Priesthoods", as Royal Advisers, as Intermediaries between the King and subject Chiefs, and as provincial Representatives of the Palace. Some of the "Ayaba" were "Wives" of the Deified King *"SANGO"* as well. Other 'wife-like' Palace delegates, known as "ILARI", served as diplomatic observers, toll collectors, messengers, cavaliers, Royal Guards, and Priests. Female "Ilari" were classified as, Wives of the King, "Ayaba".

Oral history reports that Male "Ilari", declared themselves "Wives of the King" as well.

These Ritually Transformed Male "wives", were free to move around the country at a time when many of the King's Female wives were "secluded", which may have been the very principle that required the creation and the proliferation of Male "wives".

The "Ilari" Palace Deputies, were prepared by *"SANGO"* Cult Officials, (*"Mogba"*), much in the same manner as Possession Priests and Priestesses, *"Elegun"*, (whose defining characteristic is, the <u>periodic displacement of their own 'Personal' Will</u>).

Like the male "Possession Priests", many male "Ilari" wore "*SANGO*" Cult Attire.

So closely were they identified with the Monarch's Consciousness and Will, they bore as Names various attributes, prayers, intentions and potential directives of the "Alaafin" himself. Each Monarch who came to the Throne renamed all the "Ilari" according to his preferences.

In order to invest them with the 'Royal Will', the Senior Palace Priestess of "*SANGO*", The *"IYA KERE"*, – initiated "Ilari" in her apartments. Their heads were shaved, incised, and planted with Powerful Substances (much like Initiated Priests). [It seems in the late 18th century, the "Ilari" role changed]

Babatunde (1979) writes that: "In the last quarter of the 18th century; "ALAAFIN, ABIODUN" Altered the nature of the "Ilari"; they were converted from Religious representatives, possessing indirect Religious authority, into 'Political and Economic Officers' possessing direct authority over the politics of the provinces."

[However, some writers feel it is hard to separate the "Ilari's" Religious functions under Indirect Rule of British colonization]

Partly owing to the Economic and Military changes of the transatlantic trade, the 18th century saw the increase of Non-Royal political institutions and the Decline of Royal control over the Empire. Numerous Kings reigned under this dark period of Non-Royal Chiefs' authority.

This period culminated in the long reign of "The BASORUN, GAHA", the Prime Minister who had derived his early power from control over OYO's trade corridor to the Atlantic ports.

Beginning around 1750, "Basorun, Gaha" installed and deposed successive "Alaafin" at his personal pleasure [Labisi, Awonbioju, Agboluaje, Majeogbe]. Under the pretense of defending "The Alaafin'" Honor, "Gaha" brutally suppressed provincial rulers and allowed his own Son's to rule arbitrarily all over the Empire. (Johnson, 1921)

Provincial rulers came to experience the most direct forms of Imperial Domination ever instituted. "Prime Minister Gaha" had made this political centralism possible, but the Palace finally found a person of "Royal Birth" who could take advantage of it. "ALAAFIN, ABIODUN". (1775 – 1789)

"ALAAFIN, ABIODUN" ordered the assassination of Basorun "GAHA" and the provincial rulers he had installed, replacing these with the "Ilari".

With his expanded body of "wives" = "Ayaba" (Royal wives), "Elegun" (possession Priests), "Iwefa" (eunuchs), and "Ilari" (messengers), "Alaafin Abiodun" surpassed all of his forefathers in Unifying a sprawling Empire under Direct Royal Control.

"Alaafin, Abiodun" established the Exemplary reign of the "Age of *SANGO*", by submitting the ideology and technology of that age, *SANGO's* Ancient Court, for his personal interests.

Old "OYO" was the Northernmost of the Yoruba Kingdoms. It intervened in the trade between the "Sahel" (the region of No. Central Africa, South of the Sahara Desert) and the Forest.

It was uniquely situated to make "Cavalry" a Major instrument of conquest. With the aid of "Hausa" veterinarians, "Oyo" maintained a Cavalry in the Forest Kingdoms.

"Oyo" owes much of the success of its Imperial Expansion over the southern savannah to its access to "Horses" from the North.

The "Equestrian" means of "Oyo" conquests, would imprint itself permanently on the Symbolism of

Political and Religious authority and representation in the region.

Theoretically, the "Ancient Africans" conceived The "STATE" as the Supreme Protective Society, an Organization for the Welfare of All Concerned, with an appointed group of persons responsible for its administration, and whose Offspring were to be trained in the same profession.

It is the Birthright of every person born to 'Own A Part of The State'. Therefore, Land was not purchased in the African State but given each Family, and increased as need required.

(the Western idea of one person Owning vast acreage and others paying Rent to live upon it is inconceivable to the African philosophy, since unless a man owns a part of the State it would be unthinkable that he would be expected to fight for its protection in time of war. The African knows that only a Fool would fight for something he did not own or rule).

All natural resources such as lakes, forests, minerals, etc., were State owned and therefore available to Everyone. To prevent the possibility of the State being controlled by any group of merchants or businessmen, it was proverbial (a practical concept) that

No One became more wealthy than the King or Statesmen, and should any enterprise become Too powerful, it ran the risk of nationalization. In this way the integrity of the State as a society for the protection of the general, rather than private interests, was more soundly insured.

The often heard charge that monarchial West Africa was feudal is ignorant. Landlords were non-existent. No King, Chief or Nobleman could order a war without the consent of a Council. A King did not himself lead an army, it was led by a War Lord or Generalissimo called a "Balogun".

Agriculture in which everyone was expected to engage in was not the sharecropper system, but based upon a "communalistic" pattern in which the population of a given Community formed themselves into a "commune" to plant, cultivate and harvest the crop of his neighbour. Marketing and profits were more Individual affairs. Thus, 'a system of Cooperation and Interdependence was maintained' without destroying the incentive of the individual.

The West African political system was "Communal Socialism", in which the vital means of production belonged to each separate Community, which in turn was united with a larger aggregate such as the Provincial State, which was in turn united with a Central State. With such a system so devoutly Respectful of the interdependence and Dignity of humans, 'Capitalism' with its extreme emphasis on Selfish Competition and Ambition, and where one or a small group of individuals might Control the means of Survival of the entire community, seems animal and Savage in its truest sense, and Destructive to the natural group instinct and cooperativeness, which supposedly raises man above beast.

OYO

The Reign of *"ORANMIYAN"* marked a New Phase in Yoruba History, as it witnessed the Executive Transfer of Political Power from *"ILE-IFE"* to "**OYO**", and there after, **OYO** became the "Political Headquarters" of the **Yoruba Race**, and that is where **The ALAAFIN of OYO** presides from.

According to historical studies, the "OYO" Palace is estimated to be sitting on about 640 acres. They still have excavations of the "Old Oyo Empire", and centuries after, some of the walls of the Capital of "Old Oyo" Empire, are still standing in its original form. That is a great testimony of the Architectural ingenuity of the Yoruba Race.

The Old Yoruba Empire distinguished itself in The World, with Three very distinctive and unique models.

First, it evolved a wonderfully developed Constitution, though Unwritten, the average Yoruba man is governed by strong convention.

Secondly, the Yoruba evolved a Military System that allows them to develop Weaponry. The Yorubas are the first to smith Iron and thus, they built foundries from where they also produced agricultural implements to boost food production.

Thirdly, the Yoruba Race, evolved a very practical method of Administration, by adopting the Cabinet System of governance. (If you are a good student of the evolution of the British Constitution, you'd know that the Cabinet System came about in Britain only as a matter of Temporal Expedience, it was Not by Design) So, as far back as the 16th Century, the Old "OYO" Empire developed the Cabinet System of Government. And from the Prime Minister, to "The Alaafin", and the various Divisional Heads, all tiers have their Roles and Responsibilities clearly spelt out and adhered to, with Separation of Powers and inputs for checks and balances.

The Military Command Structure is so unique that "The Aare Ona Kankanfo", as the Generalissimo of the Military, led the "Oyo" Warlords successfully to Many battles between the 13th and 16th century, that preserved the territorial integrity of the Yoruba race. During this time, OYO extended its territorial limits to Nupe, Dahomey, Abomey, Wede and other parts of Togoland, and today, these people are off-shots of the Great Yoruba Kingdom.

The ALAAFIN'S of ỌYỌ

1. Oranmiyan – Ancient Oyo built
2. Ajaka – dethroned
3. Sango – became deified as God of Thunder & Lightning
4. Ajaka – re-installed on throne
5. Aganju – long prosperous reign, tragic end
6. Kori – (Mother was Iyayun, she wore Crown and Ruled Kingdom until Kori was of age),(Ede and Osogbo built), (Timi and Gbonka)
7. Oluaso – long and prosperous reign
8. Onigbogi – evacuation of Oyo-Ile around 16th Century
9. Ofiran – built City of Saki
10. Egunoju – founder of Oyo Igboho
11. Orompoto – (Oyo Regains its Military fame)
12. Ajiboyede – (celebrated Bere Festival)
13. Abipa – 1570-1580 (Oyo rebuilt)
14. Obalokun – 1580-1600
15. Ajagbo – 1600-1658
16. Odaranwu – 1658-1660
17. Kanran – 1660-1665
18. Jayin – 1665-1670?
19. Ayibi - 1678-1690

20. Osiyango – 1690-1698
21. Ojigi – 1698-1732
22. Gbaru – 1732-1738
23. Amuniwaye – 1738-1742
24. Onisile – 1742-1750
25. Labisi – 1750 (Basorun Gaha succedded his father as Basorun and liquidated 4 Oba's, before Abiodun ascended the Throne and got rid of him)
26. Awonbioju – 1750 (130 days)
27. Agboluaje – 1750-1772 (celebrated Bere Festival)
28. Majeogbe – 1772-1775
29. Abiodun Adegolu` – 1775-1789 (Bere Celebrated)
30. Aole – (Mutiny, curse on Yoruba people)
31. Adebo – (reigned 130 days)
32. Maku – 18??-1830 (short reign, 3 moons)
33. Majotu – (Ilorin sized by the Fulani)
34. Amodo – 1830 (Oyo becomes tributary to Ilorin)
35. Oluewu – 1833-1834 (Ibadan and Abeokuta founded) (Fall of Ancient Oyo, Katunga)
36. Abiodun Atiba – 1837-1859 (Founder of present Oyo, celebrated Bere Festival)
37. Adelu – 1858-1875
38. Adeyemi I – 1875-1905
39. Lawani Agogoija – 1905-1911

40. Ladigbolu – January 1911 - December 1944
41. Adeniran Adeyemi II – January 1945 – September 1955
42. Bello Gbadegesin (Ladigbolu II) – July 1956 – 1968
43. Lamidi Olayiwola Adeyemi III – November 19, 1970-
Present Alaafin of Oyo (Adeyemi Lineage)

The First Alaafins

The "OYO ALAAFIN" is an integral portion of the Yoruba Nation that descended from the Historical figure, *"ODUDUWA"* or *"OLOFIN"*.
According to our historians, the Yoruba arrived in their present homes in waves from the Ancient **"Meroe"** of Eastern SUDAN. *"ILE-IFE"* was their First principal Centre of Civilization. *"ORANYAN"*, The First "ALAAFIN", was the grandson of *"ODUDUWA"*.
They all met indigenous populations that they conquered and assimilated. In different monarchial traditions as they arrived in waves from their Original Homes in the "SUDAN", they instituted various Kingdoms: "IFE", "OYO", "IJESA", "IJEBU", "OWU", "OWO", "EKITI", "ONDO", "KETU", etc.

As the Arrowhead of the "OYO" People and the Head of their Monarchy, the exercise of Power saw **"ORANYAN"** touching "IFE", the "EDO" Kingdom, and eventually "OYO". A fighter and a Warrior, the administration of his Kingdom came to a bloom under his sons: *"DADA AJUWON AJAKA", "SANGO", "AFONJA", "AGANJU"* (with Regent *"IYAYUN"*, a Female, when the Monarch died and before *"KORI"* came of age to rule), and *"OLUASO"*. (an area of time nearly approximating about 100A.D. to 1500A.D.)

AJAKA had two terms on the Throne before and after **SANGO**.

SANGO had several distinctions as a Monarch:
1. He shifted the Capital from *"Oko"* in the vicinity of "Ogbomoso" to *"Old Oyo"* on the famous tributary of Nigeria River, called River Moshe.
2. He established the hegemony of *"The Alaafin"* over *"The Owu"*, near "Ogboro" and in conflict; the later fled to "Iwu Ogbere", an area between "Ife" and "Ijebu".
3. **SANGO** was the product of an Intertribal marriage between a "NUPE Lady" and "The ALAAFIN".

4.   *SANGO* extended the area of The **"OYO"** **Empire**, and so was able to exercise Power over stretches of land of the Rivers "Niger" and "Ogun".

5.   The *"Osun"* and *"Oya"* Waterways were named after his Deified Wives. They represent viable religions and Deities over a wide range of Yorubaland.

AGANJU was noted for erecting 120 High Rise Gables and installing Bronze and Brass Pillars as a way of enhancing the beauty of The "OYO-ILE Palace".

OLUASO was suave, princely and blessed with about 10 Sets of Twins. Handsome and wealthy, he was the Solomon of the "ALAAFIN" Monarchy.

The Cult of *"ṢANGO"*

Blood red and bone white are the colors of the God of Thunder and
Lightning. Violence and Calm meet in his image.
(A Sango Praise Poem)

The Legend of the *"GOD of THUNDER"*,
The Great King *"SANGO"*, 4th **KING** of The
YORUBA, 3rd **"ALAAFIN"** of The Ancient City of
"OYO", is a tale of Command. "OYO" the Ancient
Political Capital of the "Yoruba", took its rise
somewhere in the 8th Century.
According to Rev. S. Johnson's account (1921):
    "OYO" was founded by *"ORANMIYAN"* a
grandson of *"ODUDUWA*, the Father of the "Yoruba"
Nation. *"ORANMIYAN"* was succeeded
by *"AJUAN, AJAKA"* who proved too mild for the
aggressive, conquering temperament of his times.
The people rejected *"AJUAN"* in favor of his more
flamboyant, warlike brother *"SANGO, OLUFINRAN"*.
    "SANGO" reigned for 7 years. He immediately
plunged the Kingdom into a series of triumphant
campaigns. He waged war against the *"Oluwo of Owu"*,
who tried to make him pay tribute after the death of

"*Oranmiyan*". He showed his bravery in battle and also his tricks. Volumes of smoke issued from his mouth and nostrils so terrifying that the "Olowu" and his army were panic stricken and were completely routed and put to flight. *"Sango"* pushed on and with every fresh victory established himself more firmly on the throne.

"Sango" was said to have the knowledge of a preparation to attract 'Lightning'. One day The Oba descended a hill call "Oke Ajaka" with some of his courtiers, slaves and cousins.

He wanted to test the preparation because he thought it had gotten damp and useless. He tried it first over his Palace. The preparation took effect, a Storm immediately gathered, and Lightning struck the Palace. Before, they could get down the hill, the buildings were on fire. Many of Sango's wives and children perished in this catastrophe.

Saddened and distraught by what had happened, and with a broken heart, he abdicated the Throne and prepared to start on a journey to his maternal grandfather, *"Elempe, King of the Nupe",* to retire.

The people of "Oyo" were saddened by the loss. They sympathized with the King and tried to prevent him by force, from carrying out his resolution. He was so overcome with grief and anger, he could not bear any opposition to his plans. He put to the sword some of his subjects who tried to stop him. They had promised to replace for him his dead wives, by whom he could beget more children, and to make good his present losses.

Determined, he set out on his journey with a few followers. His head slaves "Biri", "Omiran" and his favorite wife "*OYA*". However his followers, after a while regretted making the move and urged their master to yield to the entreaties of those citizens of "Oyo", who with all loyalty promised to replace his losses, as far as man can do, and to rebuild the Palace. But "*Sango*" was determined to go on with his plans. Seeing this, "Biri", along with all of *Sango's* followers, forsook him and returned to the city.

"*Sango*" now resented his rashness, especially when he found himself deserted by his favorite and most loyal slaves "Biri and Omiran". He could not proceed alone, and for shame he could not return home, so he resolved to end his own life.

At **"Koso"** he sat under a Shea Butter tree to contemplate how to end his life. There was 'a Flash of

Lightning, followed by a peal of Thunder and **"Sango"** Sank Slowly Into The Earth'. Some legends have it that he climbed a Silk Cottonwood tree and hung himself (which is a distortion of history).

On hearing of the King's death, "Biri" committed suicide at *Koso*, as did "Omiran". His cousins "Omo Sanda" committed suicide at *Popo*, "Babayanmi" at *Sele,* "Obei" at Jakuta and his Favorite Wife *"OYA"* at *Ira.*

Thus ended the life of this remarkable King, who ruled over all the "Yoruba", including "Benin", "Dahomey" and "Popo", and is worshipped by all the "Yoruba" race as **The GOD of THUNDER and LIGHTNING".**

In every "Yoruba" and "Popo" town to this day, whenever there is 'a flash of Lightning followed by a peal of Thunder', you will hear shouts of **"KAWO O, KABIYE SI"** (Welcome Your Majesty, Long live the King).

(another account)

"SANGO" was an Early Ruler of the **"OYO" Empire,** and He Remains a Symbol of "OYO" Royal Might.

"SANGO" was the son of "OYO's" founder, *"ORANYAN"*, by a **"Tapa"** ("Nupe") **Princess,** who was given in marriage by her father to cement an alliance between the Two Kingdoms. *"Oranyan's"* son and immediate successor *"Ajaka"* was deposed for his weakness, having submitted "OYO" to the rule of the neighboring Kingdom of "OWU".

Replacing his brother on the throne, *"Sango"* refused to render the accustomed "tribute" to the Monarch of "Owu", who then threatened, significantly, to deprive *"Sango"* of his wives and children.

Using his remarkable "Medicinal" Powers (*oogun*), *"Sango"* produced 'Smoke' from his mouth and nostrils, frightening the "Owu" King and his army into flight.

Tales report that *"Sango's"* Great Powers led him to tyranny. He is also said to have accidentally destroyed his own compound, whereupon he either abdicated voluntarily, or was forced to commit suicide.

Some of these tales are attributed to 'Christian Propaganda', thereby questioning the premise that *"Sango"* is tragically flawed and suicidal.

[**Isola, 1991:** blames this Distortion on the 'Church Mission Society School' headmaster who published the "Iwe Kika Ekerin Li Ede Yoruba" in the 1940's]

[**Abimbola, 1990:** cites the drumming renditions of the two phrases in Yoruba, to prove that *"Obaa Koso"* ("The King of Koso") Does NOT refer to suicide by hanging]

Although probably products of a 19th century Missionary Revision, *"Sango's"* Supposed tragic flaws of tyranny and inadequate control over his own power, live on in the Modern Bourgeois Distortion, popularized by Duro Ladipo's play 1964.

What appears Consistently in most tales is, that upon his death 'He Ascended to The Sky' and proclaimed his continued Power in the form of "THUNDER and LIGHTNING", the Incendiary Force with which He is identified.

"SANGO" is a Divine Prototype, a *"God"*, a *"Divinity"*, to whom all of those born with certain Fiery Proclivities may identify. He was proclaimed "King", because he can go into any situation and extract the best out of it for himself and his followers. He is able to do this because he is the "Master of Strategy and Tactics", and is, therefore, associated with Generals and Field Marshals. He has the ability to find the shortest distance between two points, in this respect he is the Master of Tacking, of going against the winds of defeat, against the odds to reach his goal.

"SANGO" loves living. He believes in Living Life to the Fullest no matter what circumstances he finds himself in, while Never Succumbing to the superficial nonsense associated with living. He is resourceful and he can live life anytime, any place and do it well.

"SANGO's" Earth Shaking **"Thunder"** speaks of his ability to move things and people, with his words of persuasiveness, the gift of gab, his quick wittiness and he can think on his feet.

He is represented by the "King" who can excite the masses with his words; the "politician" who can be everything for everyone; the "lawyer" who can win indefensible cases; a "pimp" with a large following of women; a "missionary or preacher" who can convert the masses; and the professions that deal with the 'psychological needs and the weaknesses of people'.

   "SANGO" is The *"GOD of FERTILITY"* and he rules the Testicles. The **"Rain"** is thought of as his "Semen" with which he helps carry on the progress of life. He is Total 'Maleness'. With his "Semen" he fertilizes, clears and cleans the Land, and replenishes the Rivers, Oceans and Seas. He rules the "Testicles" and wants all his children to have "balls", so much so that he recognizes no daughters, and his Female children are addressed as his "Sons".

   "SANGO" enjoys problem situations, where he can use his abilities to weigh the odds and plot a course of action.

He demands that his children be both Physically Fit and Mentally Alert in order to meet the challenges of life.

"Blood Red and Bone White" are the colors of The **"THUNDERGOD, *SANGO*"**, Violence and Calm meet in his image. The complex Deity is memorably compared to 'a cloud of locusts in the sky'. When red and white beads are worn about the neck, initiation in his Cult is communicated, as well as 'mystic alliance between "Thundergod" (red) and the "God of Creativity" (white)'. Priests wear the sign of the "Thundergod", the 'double headed axe', as a tattoo on their arm. Priests dance with a carved wooden Double-axe called *"Oshe Sango"*, each gesture a gloss on deeper meaning; each motion a materialization of Ancient Truths.

The "Double-headed Axe" is the Symbol of the "Thundergod". The Double-headed Axe as "Balanced Fire". The Double-headed Axe as suggested punishment and death, "Lightning, the Wrath of GOD." Axes with parallel horizontal marks, three on each stone suggest the marks of "The Royal Family of *"OYO"*, the Lineage of *SANGO.*"

There are probably as many styles of dancing with the "Thundergod Axes" as there are inspired Priests. Senior "Possession Priest" can dance with them. However, although the means of 'expressing the Force of the Deity in dance' Vary from Senior Priest to Senior

Priest, the informing Dualities of the 'Cool and the Hot, of Mind and Energy' seem to remain.

The marvel of the 'Thundergod Axe Tradition' is that the sculptures seem to suggest, quite often, 'the Union of the Worshipper with the Fire of the Deity'. As "Meteorites" are associated with the 'Fire from Heaven, the Lightning of *Sango*', so the suggested "Celts" upon the Head of the staff are like the sign of 'Twinned Fire, Twinned Lightning, Twinned Manifestation of *Sango's* Wrath.'

"*AFONJA*-carrying-fire-as-a-burden-on-his-head" a single metaphor tells of 'the Taming of Force by Intellect and the Human Mind'.

Some Double-headed Axe show, in the figured portion, a "woman" kneeling holding her breasts. "Thunderstones" are carved on each side of her elaborate coiffure, "Fire In Her Hair".

Only the devotee can 'master such violence without pain or danger'. The Protective Goodness of the followers of the **"Deity of Thunder, *Sango*"**, is suggested by the Holding of the Breasts, signifying human continuity. Her Respectful Kneeling is also a sign of Protection, for "the guiltless never meet the war which is waged at the back of the eyes". A Parable of 'Fire culled by Feminine Grace'.

Shrines

The *"SANGO"* Temple of "IBADAN", is the Most Striking Traditional Shrine of the city, and its Famous Screen of Carved Posts still stand since being photographed in October 1910 by Leo Frobenius who wrote: "I am bound to say that for a moments space the originality of the building in front of me….struck me dumb….a lofty, long and very deep recess made a gap in the row of fantastically carved and brightly painted columns. These were sculptured with horsemen, men climbing trees, monkeys, women, Gods and all sorts of mythological carved work. The dark chamber behind revealed a gorgeous red ceiling, pedestals with stone axes on them, wooden figures, cowry shells, hangings…the whole scene was superbly impressive". A photograph of the Temple shows the Alter. Above the lintel, are low relief representations in clay sculpture of Thundergod Axes flanking a Thundergod rattle; to the right of these motifs appears also in clay bas-relief, the ghostly outline of four panels within a square, suggesting the form of "Thundergod Leather Wallet" the *"Laba Sango"*.

Such wallets, seven of them, appear on the wall of the Alter. They function as both a receptacle for Ritual paraphernalia and as virtual hangings, recalling the Ancient Splendor of the Court of *"Aganju"*. Each wallet bears four panels in which appears a figure of a human with tailed headdress, suggesting the presence of the "Trickster God, *Esu/Legba"*. Right had up, left down, recall "Thundergod" choreography, aspects of the dance Sacred to the Deity seem framed within the Leather Panels on the wall.

The Seven *Tassels ("Amila")* at the bottom of each Wallet have been interpreted by a senior Lagosian Priest of divination as 'a sign of *"Egungun Cloth"* attached to *"Sango Cloth".*' By this he means that according to myth, the "Thundergod" once donned the varicolored appliquéd garb of the Ancestral Masquerade *("Egungun"),* a Special Costume known as *"Eku"*, when he was seriously ill at the time of an epidemic. Diviners had commanded him to wear the cloth so that he might live. It was believed that the spirits fomenting the disease would run away when they saw "cloth of the dead". The ruse worked. *Sango* wore the *"Eku"* Cloth and survived. Hence the "Thundergod" is sometimes known as *"Areku-Jaiye"*, meaning "one-who-wears-the-cloth-of-death-while-still-alive".

There is a further and powerful concordance between the Tassel and Appliqué of the *"Laba"*, and Costume worn by the Possession Priest of the Cult of "The Thundergod". *"Appliquéd Panels"* flare from the Waist of the dancer, as the Tassels appear at the bottom of the *"Laba"*.

The close connection of **"Egungun"** with **"Sango"** is to be understood as both were initially "OYO" institutions. It is claimed that **"Sango"** started the worship of *"Egungun"* as the Spirit of his Father *"ORANMIYAN"*. **"Oranyan"** is believed to have died at *"IFE"* and his body turned to stone. Stone carving and terra-cotta were means of 'Immortalizing' the Dead in life, and this is believed to be the earliest Personification of the 'Spirits of the Ancestors' in Yorubaland. **"Sango"** could not carry the corpse of *"Oranmiyan"* to *"Oyo"*. He is reported to have brought the *'Incarnated Spirit'* of **"Oranmiyan"** to **"BARA"** (the Royal Mausoleum). He installed the *"Iya-Mode"* as the Chief Priestess of *"Bara"*, and other Older Women in the Palace whom he termed *"Baba Bara"*, 'fathers to communicate the wishes of **Oranmiyan** to **Sango**,' and she was to Call **"Oranmiyan's"** Masquerade from a room called *"Ile'run"* in *"BARA"*.

Later the ceremony of 'bringing the *Spirit* of the deceased home' in the form of a Masquerade, became widespread as part of Funeral Rites of Lineages.

On the Altar of *"SANGO"* are placed Four Terra-Cotta broad-mouthed Vessels **(*"Ikoko"*)** which serve as Stands for Calabashes in which Ritual paraphernalia are stored. The most elaborate is emblazoned with base-relief representation of a 'Fish-legged Deity', flanked by devotees brandishing Thundergod Axes. The vessels often contain Ritual Water, but here serve as support for a Round Lidless Wooden Bowl *("OPON SANGO")*, in which a reclining "Twin" Statuette, an *"Ose Sango"* and Large "Thunderstones" sit. The latter elements apparently burnished with "Indigo". Here the *"Ikoko"* form surrogate wooden Mortars (*"ODO SANGO"*) in which "Thunderstones" normally are kept.

To the right of the figured *"Ikoko"* on the "Ibadan" Altar appears the carved wooden image of a seated **"Dog"**. The animal is especially associated with *"Sango"* and sometimes appears in the presence of the Priest, decked in its own Appliquéd Finery. To the right of the Dog, appears the **"Thundergod-axes"**, Large, Monumentally rendered. This particular dance sculpture must have been balanced on the Head of the dancer, for there is no handle for the conventional gripping of the wand.

In the middle of the Altar, stored in an open container, the reclining image of a "Twin", and the jutting point of the "Horns of the Harnessed Antelope" (two *"Igala"*), for ***"Orisa, Oge"***, a Deity closely associated with the "Thundergod", recalling the praise poem:

Oge malamala de!
Yio gbe o
Yio gbe omo re jeje

Orisa shining like fire, has arrived!
Oge will support you
Oge will support your child with calm.

Heard at "Ipapo", the verb *"gbe"* (support), is crucial; the Altar is called *"Agele"*, conceptually holding up the "House of The Gods"; the Terra-cotta Vessels support the emblematic "Fire of Heaven"; and the House Post carved in the form of "Warriors from Ilorin", support white Cylindrical Shafts suggestive of the "Mortar of the Thundergod".

'The Caryatids (sculptured columns) support the Roof, the Altar supports the Vessels, the Vessels the Stones.' When the *"Ose Sango"* is taken into the Dance, these themes of 'Vitality in Repose' are brought into new prominence. The *"OSE"* carries the implications of the "Alter" into the light of day, from static into motion.

The Shrine to "The Thundergod" has been interpreted as a 'Carved Retinue of *Sango*, Standing Before the Invisible Presence of *Sango* Seated On His Throne.' The Shrine of the Thundergod had been defined as a "Palace", 'The Altar His Royal Court, and the Altar Figures as Followers or Courtiers of the King.' The sculptured wooden Pedestals, *"Odo Sango"*, upon which the Thunderstones rest is "The Throne of the Deity, *Sango*", with the Support of the Stones implying the 'Majestic Presence of The Deity Himself, Seated In Glory Upon His Throne.'

In addition, the "Dance Wands" seem to embody elements of commemoration. A Legend tells of 'the Warrior Comrades of the Thundergod':
 "When *Sango* was going to war he needed strong support. He consulted "The God of Divination, *IFA*".

"IFA" gave him Two Men to be his bodyguards. One was named **"Ose"**, the second **"Sere"**. *"Ose"* carried a "Staff" into battle. *"Sere"* was holding a "Calabash", rattling it, 'invoking Supernatural Powers', whenever they were going to war. Since then forever, the **"Ose Sango"** named after the Guard, has been used by "The Thundergod", as a source of "Power" to vanquish his enemies.

The Sexuality of **"Sango"** is often spoken of. He provokes jealousy (the Praise Songs say), through the exercise of His Penis. There are photographs of an **"Ose Sango"** carved in the unmistakable image of the **"Penis"**, with Thunderstones as **"Testes"**. In this instance, the "Double-Axe" constitutes the 'Essence of the Manhood of The Deity'. All of these suggestions of "POWER"; the Sexuality of The GOD, the Memory of the Bodyguard, the Royal Line of "The ALAAFIN of OYO", Enrich the **"OSE SANGO"**.

Cults and Festivals

It is said that *"SANGO"* is one of the Most Popular and Powerful Cults among the "OYO". He is still associated with "Thunder", and therefore in "Rain" magic. Like all **Orisa**, he brings Fertility to women. One of his Special Functions is to 'kill liars and thieves'.

Normally, every fourth day is set aside for his worship. Every worshipper has his own little Shrine in his house and he begins his day with divination with the "Bitter Kolanut" (*"orogbo"*). The nuts are split in the middle and then thrown to the ground. If one half turns upwards and the other downward then *Sango*'s answer is Positive and there will be rejoicing. If on the other hand, both faces turn downward or both upwards the answer is not satisfactory and further questions will follow, "Are you angry? Are you hungry? Have I forgotten such and such a person? Is it because I quarreled with such and such a person? etc.", until a positive answer is obtained. Through further questioning, it will then be found with what sacrifice "*Sango*" can be appeased.

Since a negative position must occur fairly frequently, the true *"Sango"* worshipper must subject his mind constantly to searching inquiries, looking for possible lapses in his behavior or even in his attitude. Thus, whilst there is no preaching in the *"Sango"* Cult, and there are no commandments to be learned by heart, the Yoruba "pagan" is well known for his integrity and compares most favorably in that respect with proselytes of other religions.

Having performed his private ceremony at home, the worshipper then proceeds to a Larger Shrine belonging to an important Priest in the town where he will meet other worshippers. After further divination the older women among them will sing Praise Names (*Oriki; "Sango Pipe"*) of The God, *"SANGO"*. These *"Oriki"* go into Many Hundreds and they vary slightly from town to town. They are of interest not only because they sometimes contain Historical reference and scraps of mythology, but because they reveal a great deal about worshippers feelings towards The God and their idea of his character.

The *"SANGO"* Cult has penetrated all parts of "Yoruba" country, and "Benin". There is much solidarity among the worshippers and members travel for miles to attend each others festivals.

Oyo

A s the medieval Monarch *"SANGO"* has come to Symbolize the Power of the Kings of "OYO", his Royal Cult plays an integral role in the installation of each King of "Oyo". In the Palace of the *"Alaafin"* at "Oyo" there is a Special Priestess, the *"Iya Naso"*, who is charged with the Palace Worship of "The Thundergod, *SANGO*", and her disciple *"Iya Alaafin Iku"* is responsible for *"Sango's"* Sacred "RAM". Palace customs reach a climax at the Annual *"BEERE Festival"* when a Masked Priest said to represent *Sango's* own Ancestral Spirit *"ALAKORO"*, perambulates the Palace walls while gesticulating in his 'Robe of Blazing Red and Shining Mask of Polished Brass,' looking like a Crimson Ghost. Before each of the main gates to the Palace he 'gestures to Heaven and then to Earth to Heaven and Earth,' and moves to the next point of Blessing.

As practiced in "Oyo", the following is the process to be gone through at the Initiation of anyone into the Mysteries of *"Sango"* Worship:

The Priests demand a **"Ram"**, a water bird called *"Osin"*, a Tortoise, a Snail, an Armadillo, a large Rat called *"Okete"*, a Toad, a Tadpole, the *Otutu* and *Opon* Beads, the Red Tail of a Parrot, a Guinea Fowl, Shea Butter, Salt, Palm Oil, the flesh of an Elephant, Venison, the *Tete* green, the Leaves of the evergreens called *Etiponla*, *Odundun* and *Iperegun* Tree, a small Knife called *"abe-Esu"*, a White Country Cloth of 10 breadths, a Mat called *"fafa"*, the Pith of Bamboo Palm Branches, and the Carriage Fees.

The Leaves are bruised in a bowl of water, and with the Infusion the candidate is 'Purified'. He or she is seated on a "Mortar" and shaved. The birds and tortoise are killed and their Hearts taken out and with slices of the Flesh of all the animals above mentioned, are pounded together with the evergreens, and a "BALL" is made of the compound. The candidate now submits to Incisions on his Shaved Head, and 'the Ball of pounded articles is rubbed into the incisions'. After the Rituals and Ceremonies are completed, the neophyte then becomes a recognized Initiated Devotee of The Deity, ***"SANGO"***.

Ede

In *"EDE"* the Annual Festival of **"SANGO"** takes place towards the end of the Rainy Season. The precise date is always announced Eighteen Days in advance, and this announcement is in itself a Minor Festival. The **"TIMI of EDE**, His Royal Highness" sits in state in his Palace and the **"Sango"** worshippers dance the famous *"Lanku"* Dance. It is a vigorous dance which is always played by the *"Lanku Bata"* Drums which are Sacred to **"Sango".** Whenever, the *"Lanku"* is played **"SANGO"** must Manifest Himself, that is to say, he must 'take possession of one of the worshippers'. As soon as the presence of *"The GOD, SANGO"* is noticed in one of them, the worshippers break off the dance and quietly lead him away.

A woman then steps forward and announces to the spectators that the Festival is to start in eighteen days.

In "Ede", the **"ALAAFIN, SANGO"** **Festival** lasts for Seven Days. It starts in the morning with various Ceremonies connected with **"Rain"** Magic. It is absolutely essential that "No Rain" should fall during these seven days. What this means can only be realized if it is remembered that 'the Ceremonies take place toward the end of the Rainy Season' when *Thunderstorms* are the rule during the afternoons. Whatever the reason, it must be stated that in successive years *Rain* has never interfered with the Ceremonies. The women go in procession to The River, and at a special place a "Calabash" containing Special Medicines is sunk into the depths. From that day onward 'the level of the River is supposed to go down and the Dry Season is to begin.'

In successive years the Dry Season has, in fact, commenced with 'The Sinking of the Calabash.' While this Ceremony takes place, the "TIMI of EDE" proceeds in Great Pomp to a place near the River to meet the worshippers. He rides under the State Umbrella and is accompanied by a huge crowd as well as by a large orchestra of Drummers and Royal Trumpeters.

In the afternoon of that day the Women of the Palace gather together to perform an Unusual Music, which is played only Once a year. They start with the Praise Names of "*SANGO*", then go to the First "TIMI", the founder of the town, and continue through the last of Twenty-two Rulers until they come to the Present King.

It is the Accompaniment, on this occasion, that is unusual. Women **Do Not** Play Drums in Yorubaland, Nor do they Hire any professional Drummers on 'This Occasion', as they may do for Other Ceremonies. Instead, **'They beat out a rhythm on Calabashes'.** Two large "Mortars" normally used for pounding yams are filled with "Water", and then 'Each Half Calabash are Beaten with a Stick to produce a hard Rhythm.' Six other women are sitting around a Very Large Calabash that is lying on the ground, and 'they Beat It with the Palms of their Hands, thus producing a softer sound.' The third "instrument" used to produce rhythm on this occasion is the **"*Sere Sango*"** Rattle. It is this Gourd filled with seeds normally used to accompany prayers.

During the rest of the week, the **"*Sango*"** worshippers give performances of dance and tricks before the "TIMI". A huge crowd gathers in the Marketplace, but the performances are really meant for The God **"*SANGO*"** Himself rather than for the human audience. The **"*Sango*"** worshippers are extremely conscious of the God's tragic nature and they desire on this occasion to entertain him and make him happy.

The principle performer must each day "carry" The God, that is to say, he must fall into an induced state of Possession, during which he will Speak with the

Voice of **"SANGO"**. He dances with incredible energy whilst in this state and appears to be Insensitive to Pain. In "EDE", this state of Possession is induced in the following manner;

The Chief Performer, **"Baba Elegun"**, takes a bundle of dry grass and lights it with a match. While dancing around in a circle, followed by other worshippers, he blows into the smoldering grass.

When at last the flames shoot up from the grass, a trembling runs throughout his body. His eyes widen and he begins to reel. **"SANGO"** has Mounted His Head. The other worshippers support him and take him away. He then puts on a 'Special Dress, which must only be worn in a State of Trance.'

He is now the 'Human Representation' of The GOD, **"SANGO"**, and when he returns dancing, he is indeed Changed. He has acquired some of the God's Superhuman Strength and Energy. He now begins his amazing performances. A favorite feat is to push an Iron Rod through his Tongue, or drive a Knife into his Flesh without flinching. One performer had an Iron Rod as thick as a little finger pushed underneath his Eyeball, and another man then Beats It with a Mallet. Another was Shot in the mouth with a Dane Gun at short range.

Strangely and charmingly these Extraordinary Feat are interspersed with Native Parlor Tricks, such as the changing of paper money into pound notes with the help of a specially constructed *Wallet*. To a European mind, such a mixture of the trifling and sublime may be illogical, but not so to the **"Sango"** worshipper, 'who wants to Accept and to Live the Whole of Life with its Greatness and it Freaks.'

These performances continue for Seven Days in the Marketplace, in front of The "TIMI" and all his Chiefs. On one occasion, however, a **"Sango"** performer showed the freakish side of his character. While everyone is expecting the *"Elegun"* to start with his performance, he suddenly appears carrying feces in a calabash. With this he goes from Chief to Chief and will not move until he has been paid some money.

"SANGO" **Festival** is concluded on the Seventh Day with a Procession of **"Fire"**. One of the worshippers carries a 'Large Pot on His Head in which is burning a **"Sacred Flame"**.' This "Flame" must be carried so that the Blessing of **"SANGO"** can be brought to All Parts of The Town.

The **Fire** is brought to The "TIMI" in the Marketplace. It is late in the afternoon and everyone is waiting for the appearance of the dancers carrying the Burning Pot.

The Sky is black with "Thunder Clouds". The atmosphere is at its most heavy and a Great Storm seems inevitable. Nevertheless, the *"Sango"* Priests seem unperturbed. They quietly shake their heads when bystanders show their anxiety. When the dancers finally appear, 'Lightning Tears the Sky.' But, No Rain Falls. Throughout the night the Rain Clouds swirl overhead, but Not A Drop comes down. The Ceremonies are Carried Out Successfully to the end.

Ibadan

The Annual Festival to *"The Alaafin SANGO"* in "IBADAN", prior to the Ceremonies, the following are collected for the Offering to *"Sango"*: *"orogbo"* Bitter Kola nut, Kola Nut, Alligator Pepper, a RAM, a Cock, *"awun"* (Tortoise), *"ewire* and *irere"* (two species of Turtles), rats, fish and maize wine. For the Priest's *"Yeri"* (a ceremonial garment) which is tied around the waist and which comes down below the knees, a piece of cloth is cut. Cowry Shells are tied on the edge and on various parts of the garment. The Cloth and a Cap to which Cowry Shells are attached are then Dyed Red with Camwood.

On the First Morning of the Ceremony, various Leaves are squeezed into water, and the water is then used to wash the **"Thunderstones"**. While the "Thunder Stones" are being washed, several Priests Shake Rattles and, Chant Verses 'In Praise of *SANGO.*' The "Stones" are then placed in a Wooden Vessel.

During the first evening of the ceremony, Bitter Kolanuts, alligator peppers, and kolanuts are brought to *SANGO*'s Shrine. Kolanuts are broken. The tips of two Bitter Kolanuts are bitten off and the remaining middle portion is cut in halves and tossed up. If one faces up and one down, the offering has been accepted. One half is put on the Shrine, the other half in the water. Kolanuts are also broken and thrown in this way, with two haves placed on the Shrine and the other two in the water, an Alligator Pepper is chewed and spit into the vessel of water. Snails are also offered to *"Sango"* and the water from them is poured in front of the Shrine. A Knife which has been held in a glowing Fire is used to cut open the Foul's mouth and its blood is poured on the Shrine.

A **"Thunderstone"** is put in the mouth of the **"Ram"** and tied there so that the animal cannot open its mouth. The Priest, as well as other participants, touch the Ram's Head with Their Heads, signifying that the "Ram" will die instead of human beings.

The red hot Knife is used to sacrifice the "Ram" and its blood is poured on the Shrine and on the ground In Front of the Shrine. The Ram's Skin is removed, and the Head, part of the Chest, Liver, Lungs, part of the Intestine, and the Heart are cooked together. The

Cooked Offering is placed in front of "*Sango's* Shrine", and a bowl of "*gbegiri*" (beans soup) is poured on the offering, as is soup from green leaves, and Okra soup. Maize Wine is poured on the Meat, and a Calabash is placed over it. Then a Bitter Kolanut is used to ask "*SANGO*" if he is satisfied. When "*Sango*" indicates his Acceptance of the Offering the participants dance around the compound, returning to eat and drink. All of the meat offered to The "*ORISA SANGO*" is removed and Eaten by members of the group.

One informant said that anyone who has been involved in wrong doing should NOT Eat This Meat. If he does, it is believed that he will be found out, or he will die.

At some point, the Priest leads the worshippers in a procession around the town. Usually five or six people get Possessed by "*Sango*" during a ceremony. Such persons make considerable noise, and Palm Oil and Blood mixed together are given to them to Calm Them Down.

On the Seventh and Last Day of the Ceremony, all the remnants on the Shrine are removed and taken to The River. Rattles and Drums are used on the march which ends the Annual Ritual.

Oshogbo

In "OSOGBO", as seen on the Eve of the Annual Festival to *"SANGO"*, an Old Woman from the *"Sango"* Cult passes through every quarter of the town, carrying the *"Sango* **Calabash"** loaded with the Symbols of **"The GOD of THUNDER,** *SANGO"*. She is accompanied by *"Bata"*, the *"Sango* **Drum"**, and Great Ceremony.

The passing of the *"Calabash"* signifies an "Open Day" in the town, when a 'stranger may take anything he needs to eat without charge.'

In a Special Chamber in the *"ATAOJA, OBA of OSOGBO"* Compound, the Priests of *"Sango"* have already started Chanting and Dancing and making Sacrifices to the *"ORISA, SANGO"*.

It appears that *"Sango"* has a Liking for a Party, for though the Priests may sing, dance and feast right through the night, 'none of them must take as much as one wink of sleep before daybreak.' One old man present explained that "these Ceremonies were trying to make the **"Thundergod"** forget his unhappy past and to put him in a Pleasant Frame of Mind for the New Year."

While the Priests are getting warmed up outside the room Enshrining the *"ORISA SANGO"*, The **"Ataoja"** and the Senior Chief of his compound sit in the Reception Room of the "Afin" (Palace) and listen to the Virtues and Powers of **"The OBA, *SANGO"*** as recounted by a Professional Praise Singer, 'who Heralds His Approach with the Clash of Iron Clappers.' He is something More than a staff sycophant (flatterer), for running through the list of 'Virtues and the Known Achievements of The Past,' is a thread of "Prophesy" a hint of 'what may be expected in the New Year.' The words are received with some solemnity, and each pronouncement is received with the smile or frown it merits. Each Prophetic Item is evoked by a Crescendo of Clashing Iron, and a state of self hypnosis is certainly 'induced in some of the audience if not in the speaker.'

The Entertainment Proper, though for the express benefit of **"*Sango"***, is enjoyed by as many of the townspeople who can squeeze into the Courtyard of the **"Oba, Ataoja"** Compound.

A Second show is later given in the "Marketplace", for though the crowd in the Palace was Great, more than one thousand of those present were actually Residents of the Royal Compound, and only a very few of the townspeople found it physically possible to get in.

In the Marketplace, the **"*ORISA SANGO*"** is exhibited to the people and the **"*Sango*"** Priests perform Magic for the Amusement of the **"Thundergod"**. Dancers, strong men, stilt dancers and conjuring are the Main Items on the program. The Priests specialize in Conjuring and in some considerable Feats of Strength.

When The **"*Ataoja*"** and His Court had returned to the "Afin", and the **"*Sango*"** Priests had started another night outside the Shrine of the **"*ORISA SANGO*"**, the townspeople started Their Own Celebration in the "Marketplace" and Drumming went on through the night.

Oyotunji
(African Village, U.S.A.)

As observed in 1979 in the "Village of OYOTUNJI" the Annual Festival for *"SANGO,* **GOD of THUNDER & LIGHTNING"** is Celebrated during the Dry Season under the sign of Leo. Priests and worshippers gather from All Over the United States. They come to Celebrate this "Great Deified King", who's Festival is full of Grand Pageants, Feasts, Music, Drumming, Dancing and Magic.

The day before the beginning of The Festival, the Traditional "RAM" is sacrificed to the *"ORISA SANGO"* along with birds and other animals Sacred to Him, and *"ESU/ELEGBA"* is given a "Goat". Chanting and drumming is heard through the night as his worshippers prepare for the next days activities.

Moments before Daybreak the worshipers gather for a procession to 'cleanse the Town of any negativity or witchcraft in the atmosphere.' They take with them a fowl, sacred water, incense, and rattles on their rounds through the Village, cleansing and purifying the town for the beginning day of the *"SANGO* **Festival"**.

The Afternoon of the First Day, the *"Egungun"* of the Temple of **SANGO, "ALAKORO"**, is brought out and is Paraded Around the Town, leading the *"Egungun"* of Each *"Orisha* Temple", who 'Represent All The Priests who have Passed On to a Higher Plane.' They are given offerings, gifts and entertainments by the Towns Civic Societies and Organizations, and the *"Egungun"* Give Their Blessings for The Festival and The Coming Year.

The Evening of the first day is given over to *"Elegba, God of Mischief"*, Merrymaking, Luck and Misfortune. Since *"Elegba"* must be placated so that everything can run smoothly, he is given a Fowl along with other offerings, while the Children, the worshippers of *"Sango"* and the townspeople, dance and frolic late into the night.

Late in the Morning of the Second Day, "The Sacred Vessels" which hold the Sacred Stones and Emblems of *"SANGO"*, are taken in a Procession around the Town escorted by the Priests and worshippers of The GOD, singing, chanting and dancing as they visit each *"ORISA* Temple" and pass every Compound. Shortly after, a drum is sounded for everyone to assemble in the Courtyard of the *"Sango*

Temple" for the Entertainments that will be given to *"OBA SANGO"* by the Towns People.
This is the same evening the Annual Play,
"The Legend of *SANGO"* by Her Ladyship, **"The** *Iya Sango",* Ayobunmi Sangode; is performed by the Members of His Temple. It is a beautiful moving Play of the Life and Tragic End of the Great Monarch, **"The ALAAFIN of OYO,** *SANGO".* Parties, feasts, drumming and dancing end the second night of the Festival.

The morning of the Third Day of The Festival is spent cooking and preparing food for the *"Gbemileri"* (High *Bata* Drum Ceremony) and Feast for *"SANGO".* Much food is cooked, for the members of the Temple of *"Sango"* must Feed the Townspeople, and All Guest that come to Celebrate the **"Festival of** *SANGO".*
"Amala" must be prepared for **"The GOD,** *SANGO",* and his special guests will be served some of this dish, "His Favorite food".
Other dishes are prepared that The God Likes, and his guests will eat and drink while enjoying the entertainments of this Special Day.

The *"Gbemileri"* begins in the early evening. A drum is sounded to call everyone to the Courtyard of

The Temple of "SANGO, God of Thunder and Lightning".
At The Temple, the Priests and worshippers are dressed in their Traditional *"Sango"* Attire, chanting, drumming and singing for *"Kawo Kabiyesi, SANGO"* to Come Join Them for His Celebration.
After the guests have arrived and, *"The OBA of OYOTUNJI, OSEIJEMAN E. A. ADEFUNMI I"*, and his entourage arrive, the chanting, singing and drumming continues as each Cult or Temple give special gifts, and Entertain **"The GOD, SANGO"** with dances, plays, skits, poetry, new songs and magic tricks. Praises are chanted and sung to *"SANGO"* by his worshippers and dances are done In His Honor. Food and drinks are served, while everyone joins in this Celebration that ends The Annual Festival for *"SANGO"*, for the year.

The devotees of *"Sango"* in "OYOTUNJI" African Village, celebrate his special day on Thursday. After they commence worshipping at their Personal Shrines, they gather at the Main Temple in "The **Afin**" to Worship *"OBA SANGO"*. They may on some Thursdays bring his Favorite Foods, or offerings of a "Ram", red roosters, guinea fowl, turtles, and quails.

They bring **"Amala"** (made from *"elubo"* yam flour), Lamb stew made with peppers, okra, palm oil, tomatoes and cornmeal; black-eye peas, okra, *"eko"*, yams, rice, sweet bananas, green plantains, red apples, peppers, and palm oil.

They bring candles, *"orogbo"* (Bitter Cola), cigars, rum, red and white wine, and incense. They bring Gifts of Brass and Gold; cedar pine, and Cloth in the colors of red and white, gold, leopard skin and royal blue and purple. They bring bags and bags of 'Money Cowries to Adorn His Shrine, and they Sing, Dance and Entertain **"OBA SANGO"** on His Special Day.'

"KAWO, KABIYESI"

"ṢANGO" INITIATION
[from an Observation seen in "Igboho" Nigeria]

{Taken from an Observation in "IGBOHO" in 1988, of Two Initiations (a Male and a Female); they differ Greatly from Samuel Johnson's brief account in, *The History of the Yoruba,* based on late 19th Century testimony in "OYO", Nigeria}

No "OYO"-Yoruba *"SANGO"* Initiation is available in writing, for the *"SANGO"* Priesthood is hedged in by *"asiri awo"* (religious secrets). At the same time, the spirit of Secrecy competes with the principle of showing others that 'There Is a Secret' and making clear 'Who Is Privileged to Know It.' While there are 'phases of the Initiation' that the "Initiate's" kinfolk, neighbors, friends, and wives or husbands, as well as investigators, are "Forbidden" to Witness; there are parts of the Ceremonies where family, and the public are expected.

In a *"SANGO"* Initiation there are usually no procedural differences for a Male or Female, Either Sex is called an *"Iyawo"* (bride) of The GOD, as in Most *Orisa* Initiations.

Two terms are used to describe initiation into the "OYO"-Yoruba "Possession Religions":
"*DOSU*" and "*SE ORISA*"
"*dosu*" = "to create *osu* [a ball of sacred substances] onto the Initiate's head."

"*se orisa*" = "to do, or make, the God", implying that human Ritual effort is required to create a "GOD" in the Initiate's body.

The Key Participants in "*SANGO*" Initiation are:

SANGO;   the Tutelary "GOD of the OYO Kingdom"

ESU;   the mischievous "GOD of Communications", The Lord of the Crossroads.

IYAWO;   "bride" or "wife", the male or female initiate and young Possession Priest.

MOGBA;   Non-Possession Priests officially responsible for the initiations of Possession Priests.

ELEGUN;   mature Male or Female Possession Priests.
A Male *"Elegun"* is the Head of the Possession
Priesthood.

IYALE;   Senior co-Wife, the Female *Elegun* who takes
care of the initiate in the *"Sango"* Shrine.

Drummers, Audience, Supplicants; The *"IYAMI"*,
women with the Power *("Aje")* to help their allies and,
to kill their enemies.

[A Possession Priests Death]

"SANGO ku ku; esin re lo n lo sorun"
"SANGO does not die; his Horse is the one who goes to
the other world"

Most *"SANGO"* "Possession Priests" are recruited from
either side of a retiring, or deceased Possession Priests
("Elegun") kindred. When a "Horse" prepares to go to
"ORUN" (Heaven, the Other World), a Sacred
(immaterial) "head load" (*"ASE"*) must be withdrawn
from his Head, and "tied onto the head" (*di nnkan ru*)
of his nominated or approved successor.

If the Priest's successor has Not been prepared before his death, the *"EGBE SANGO"* removes the "load" from the Head of the "deceased Priest", but delays the burial until a suitable successor is approved.

Priestly recruitment Does Not Always follow in "Hereditary" Lines. Some have been spoken to through "divination"; some "signs" may be seen at birth; illness or misfortune may be interpreted through divination as a "calling"; some Children are said to have "brought the *ORISA* from the Other World", just as people 'bring their *Heads* from Heaven.'
Such cases, as these infants, are usually attributed to Inheritance from some forgotten Ancestor.

The Important Phases of the *"idosu"* Initiation can be spread out over a Year, but the "Focus" of events is a period of 14 days, when the "initiate", sleeps with his or her Female caretaker in the domestic Shrine of a *"MOGBA SANGO"*.

During the First Seven Days of Initiation, the "initiate" is considered as, and treated as a "Newborn". He or She is shaved bald, and is nude or semi-nude as a newborn Baby.

He or She sleeps in the Shrine Room with a woman who is called The *"IYALE"*, who bathes him/her and attends to all this "Infants" bathroom functions.

The Ritual Attendant (*"Iyale"*) feeds him/her, and ensures that all food has been properly cooled.

Whenever the "Newborn" leaves the Shrine room, he/she must wear over his/her Head a "White Cloth" associated with *"ORISA NLA*, The God Who Forms Fetuses In The Womb".

The wearing of the Head Cloth and being in the Shrine Room implies that the Shrine room is, for the Newborn, like a "WOMB". The Female Ritual Attendant (*"IYALE"*), for the first "Seven Days", is the Newborn Initiates "Mother".

Therefore, at the Public Presentation of the New Initiate (Iyawo) on the "Seventh Day" is called *"iko omo jade"* = "The carrying outdoors of the child", (after the name of the First "Official" Public appearance of a Newborn Baby Girl. Newborn Boys are on the 9th day, Newborn Girls are on the 7th day).

The scheduling of Initiations, assimilates the New "Initiate" specifically to a Baby Girl, the "*Iyawo*", Male or Female, is the "BRIDE" of The GOD.

The *"SANGO"* initiate begins residence in the Shrine Room (*"gbongan"*) on the <u>EVE of the "First Day"</u>, after Offering's have been given to the grave of the diseased predecessor. Money is circulated around the initiates head and deposited on the grave.

In the *"MOGBA's"* house, chewed Kola Nuts (*Obi & Orogbo*) and the blood of a freshly sacrificed chicken are applied to various parts of the body of the initiate in order to 'feed the "GOD" inside him/her' and to Strengthen those body parts.
The Female Ritual Attendant (*"Iyale"*) Prays, placing the chewed (*Orogbo*) kolanut:
On the palms of the initiate's hands:
"A maa gbowo to daa"
(We will get a lot of money),
On the abdomen:
"Kaa ma ri inu run"
(May we not get a runny stomach)
On the sides:
"OLORUN do nii je kaa ri iku, e jowo"

81

(God will not let us die, please)
On the forehead:
"Koorii re o ma buru; koori re o ma fo"
(Your 'head' should not go bad; [become crazy, stupid]
you should not get headaches)

The "initiate" and all the *"Sango"* Priests stay awake
that night. The "initiate" drinks a preparation containing
"special herbs", and is bathed in herbal infusions.
A Priest then shaves the "initiates" head. Incisions are
made on the scalp, to better allow the penetration of the
"Sacred Force" that is being inserted there.
The "initiate" sits on an "overturned Mortar", while
numerous animals are then sacrificed to his/her Head
in a Rite called *"afejewe"*.
(The blood may be painted on with the Feather of a
Vulture *"igun"*)
"SANGO" then "mounts" *(gun)*, or possesses, his New
"Iyawo" (bride).
From this day until the end of the *Iyawo's* residence in
the Shrine room, the initiate is fed, bathed, and led
around like a child.

In the Morning of the "FIRST DAY", a combination of Kola Nuts *(obi)*, Bitter Kola *(orogbo)*, and Alligator Pepper *(Atare)* is chewed by a Priestess and, along with other ingredients, is applied in a ball called *"OSU"* to the initiates head, on the "incision". Using the "Vulture Feather", the Priestess paints White and Red designs and "Lightning" on the initiates head with blood-colored "camwood" *(osun)* and white "chalk" *(efun)*.

The *"OSU"* ball and painted designs will be washed off, and replaced on the *"iyawo's"* head at least twice a day for the balance of the First 7days in the Shrine room.

On the Morning of the "First Day", the initiate carries Offerings on their head to the "Crossroads" for the *"ORISA ESU"*, Divine Messenger & Trickster", and for the *"IYAMI"* *("Aje")*.

Iyawo's Female Ritual Attendant, the *"Iyale"*. always leds *Iyawo* to the Crossroads. The initiate, his *"Iyale"*, and other Priests will dance in a circle at the Crossroads, [which may also be the location of the Deceased Possession Priests 'Grave' as well]. Whether or not the grave is there, the "Crossroads" is a 'Point of Contact with *The DIVINE.*'

On the "SECOND DAY", the Priests, who have again spent the night with the initiate, awake and chant the *"Oriki"* (Praise Poetry) of several of the *"ORISA"*. On the EVE of the 'Third Day', the Priests Divine with Cowry Shells, *"SANGO's Will"* in relation to his *"Iyawo" (won te Orisa fun iyawo)*, and to determine the bride's *("iyawo's")* Taboo's *("eewo")*. They also tie the Special Bead Necklaces called *"kele"* (*"ileke"*) on the bride.

On the Morning of the "THIRD DAY" the *"Iyawo"* bears an Offering to The Crossroads for the *"IYAMI"*, and another to The River for *"SANGO"*[the writers observations in "Brazil" Rituals]; {In other schools *ORISA, "OSUN"*}. At The River, the *"iyawo"* and Priests bathe.

In the Afternoon of this "Third Day" the Priests publicly perform vulgar and funny acts and songs, and dance to the beat of the *"Bata"* Drums.
Then begins a serious "Circle Dance". During this "Circle Dance", the New Bride *("Iyawo")*, wearing Cult Clothing, and his/her female Ritual Attendant, the *"Iyale"*, are "Mounted" by *"SANGO"*.
The audience contributes money to the Mounted *"SANGO's"* attendants, and to the holders of Important

Ritual Implements, such as the Sacred Pouch, *"LABA SANGO"*, used to contain *"SANGO's"* Emblems and "THUNDER AXES".

Until the <u>EVE of the "Seventh Day"</u>, the *Iyawo* remains in or near the *"Mogba's"* rooms and continues the "infant" care, feeding and bathing routine, administrated by the Ritual Attendant *("Iyale")*.

On the EVE of the "Seventh Day", more animals are sacrificed, and some of their blood, mixed in with the Sacred Herbal concoction, is drunk. The *"iyawo's"* head is re-shaved, leaving an area of stubble, which is then darkened with Indigo.

On the Morning of the "SEVENTH DAY", a "RAM" that has remained in a Special place on the compound next to the Shrine is brought out, and its forehead is pressed a number of times to that of the *"Iyawo"*.

The "Ram" is then sacrificed, along with several chickens. The blood is collected in a bowl and Priest taste a bit of its contents.

[The Observer is asked to leave for the afternoon at this point in the ritual]

{The blood is then applied to the *"Iyawo's"* head. *"SANGO"* Initiations require the "bathing of the Newborn initiate in blood" – *"afejewe"*. A vast quantity of animal blood is used in the initiation, Particularly the sacrificing and transference of blood from *"SANGO's"* Emblematic animal – the "RAM" – to form the "Blood Ties", where the initiate becomes a 'Mighty Kinsman of The Royal House of *"SANGO"*.'}

More offerings are borne on the *"iyawo's"* head to the Crossroads for *ESU,* The *IYAMI,* or the Dead *ELEGUN.*

The *"Iyawo"* is then seated Outside on a Mortar and surrounded by the Priests and their Curtain of wrap skirts (*iro*). After two chickens are sacrificed within the enclosure, the *Iyawo* comes out staggering.
The audience sings and signs with its hands that *"SANGO"* should not kill anyone as he arrives from the Other World. [the observer says that a second such ceremony was performed later on the same day in one of these initiations]

On the Afternoon of the "Seventh Day", another Public Ceremony takes place. It is called *"iko omo jade"* (the carrying outdoors of the child). The *"Iyawo"* is dressed wearing the "CULT" Clothing.
{Whether Male or Female, the New *"Iyawo"* (Bride) wears the Cult Attire = *iro* (wrapped cloth), *buba* (shirt/blouse) and *oja* (cloth worn over shoulder or for carrying a small child), including a textile paneled skirt *"Aso Eku"* covered with images}

Before the *"Iyawo"* emerges for his/her 'First Appearance as an Initiated Member of the Priesthood', the female Ritual Attendant *(Iyale)* washes *iyawo's* feet at the threshold of the *MOGBA's* house, where the *iyawo* has resided for the past seven days. {The "initiate" has Officially outgrown the status of Infant of the house before truly entering the Priesthood.

The Transformation of the Infant into an "*Iyawo*" occurs expressly on the "Seventh Day"}

The Priests of the Cult dance in a Circle playing miming sexual acts and laughing. This playful acting ends abruptly, the drums speed up, 'the Dance Circle Spins Like a Cyclone', and The GOD "*SANGO*" simultaneously "mounts" his "*Iyawo*" and Senior co-Wife.

Senior male Priest rotate money, given by the crowd, around the "*Iyawo's*" head and place it in front of the drums. Two Possession Priest are then "mounted" – one Male and one Female – and the "*SANGO*" Manifest God's, dance.

The "*SANGO*" Manifest in the Male Priest, [at the ceremony being observed], climbs onto an overturned Mortar to display himself to the crowd. Members of the crowd again give money to the *Manifest God* "*SANGO's*" attendants, and to the bearers of important Ritual Implements.

Members of the audience then Bare Their Heads, to receive 'Blessings of The GOD's Touch', for Fertility, Health, and Wealth.

Later that day the *"Ewo"* (taboo) of the *"Iyawo"* is announced, and the people are invited to 'pay a fee for the privilege of violating it, for One Last Time.'
[In the 2 cases witnessed the "taboo" forbids anyone to Strike the Priest]. The audience members were given a piece of straw with which to hit the *"Iyawo"* as he sits on the mortar.
Suddenly, "The GOD, *SANGO"* mounts the *"Iyawo"* and leaps up, enraged. Priests restrain the *Manifest "GOD"* and lead him into the *"Mogba's"* apartment, where the *"Iyawo"* is called back to consciousness.
In the succeeding days, the Special Necklaces *("kele")* remain around the *"Iyawo's"* neck, and his circle of stubble left on his head, is kept darkened with Indigo.

On the "TWELFTH DAY" of the Initiation, the Male *"Iyawo"* [being observed] followed by drummers and Priestly attendants, parade around the Town wearing the Cult Attaire and Beads, and carrying in his hand a Switch, *"atori" or "pason"*, to fight against the *"AJE"* (Witches).
The "Twelfth Night", will be the Last Night that the *"Iyawo"* spends with the female Ritual Attendant *"IYALE"* in the *"MOGBA's"* apartment Shrine room.
{Taken from an Observation in "IGBOHO" in 1988}

The THUNDERGODS
"The *Xevioso*"

*X*EVIOSO was brought to "Abomey", Dahomey from "Xevie". Before he was known by this name, he was called "*SO*". "*Xevioso*" is also known as "*AGBOLESU*" (Ram-Great-Male), since he and the "RAM" the Symbol of the "THUNDERGODS", are held to have the same form.

"*MAWU*, The Creator Divinity", is called "*SOGBO*" by the "*Xevioso*" followers. "*SOGBO*" is therefore the "Greatest of All Gods", but She appointed Her Son, "*AGBE*" the exercise of Direct Control over what occurs in The Universe.

"*AGBE*, Ruler of The Earth", corresponds to "*LISA*" of the "Sky Pantheon". He is charged with the Care of "The Earth". "*Agbe*" came to Earth to fulfill the Mission given him by "*SOGBO*", and for him "The SEA" was created as a place in which to reside.

When "*Agbe*" came down from on high to live in The Sea, his Sister/Wife, "*NAETE*", came with him. Like her husband, "*NAETE*" lives in The SEA, but She has a "River" in which she rests.

She bore to "*Agbe*" the following children: *Agboyu, Axwaga, Tokpodun, Saxo, Gbeyogbo*, and *Afrekete*. After "*Agbe*" had established himself in The Sea, he continued to communicate with "*SOGBO*" at the point where Sea and Sky Meet (The Horizon). It is said that "*Agbe*" and his children are both in The Sky and The Sea, because 'Their Home is where Sea and Sky Meet.' And that is why when a person dies he must 'Give an Account of His Life to the Ruler to whom the Earth was entrusted.'

The Eyes of "*Agbe*" are seen in The SUN Rising in the Morning, and in The Evening returning home.

"*SOGBO*" bore other children after "*AGBE*", and these other children were vested Control of "The SKY". The Sky is called "*DJI*", and is a thousand times Greater than The Earth. The Children born after "*AGBE*" are: *Aden, Akolombe, Adjakata, Gbwesu, Akele, Alase*, and *Gbade*.

These Deities busy themselves with the affairs of "The SKY", as "*Agbe*" and his children do in "The SEA". But "*SOGBO*" Supervises the behavior of All of them, and watches over the "Rainfall" of The Earth. "*Agbe*" was told that when "Rain" was needed, 'Water was sent Up from The SEA, and when this Water had mounted almost to The Sky, "*SOGBO*" would "SHOUT", and

"Rain" Would Fall.' Through the "Rainfall" she sees that justice is rendered On Land. When a Ship is struck by "Lightning" it is said to be the work of *"Agbe"*, but when it strikes on The Land it is the work of *"SOGBO"* and Her Children in The SKY.

The DEITIES Who RULE OVER The SEA

"AGBOYU", the first son of *"AGBE"* and *"NAETE"* watches over his mother.

"AXWAGA", is very brutal. He tries to out do his father. A doer of evil, he causes all the boats to sink. When his father saw how much trouble he made, he ordered *"Axwaga"* to Leave The Sea and settle elsewhere. He established himself at *"Xevie"*. He had no peace there, for the people kept annoying the remarkable stranger. He changed himself into a Great "River" called *"Axwaga"*, which makes 'a Noise Almost As Loud As The Sea.'

"TOKPODUN", she is identified with *"YALODE"*, 'Goddess who Women Especially Worship.' She is quite, well-behaved and beloved of her mother. She was so dismayed by the brutality of her brothers that she left the parental home in The Sea and

established herself not far from *"Whydah"*, becoming a "River".

"SAXO", inhabits the Incoming Waves, and it is he who Makes The Sea Rise.

"GBEYOGBO", is the God of the Receding Surf. He is said to be the most evil of The Sea Deities, since the most dangerous part of the travel by Sea known to the "Dahomeans" is the launching of their boats through the heavy surf.

"Agbe" holds *"Gbeyogbo"* in High Esteem, and to him is assigned all the Authorized Drowning of men and Sinking of Ships.

"AFREKETE", is the Youngest Child of *"Agbe"* and *"Naete"*. She is the Most Favored of the children and is likened to *"Legba"* playing the role of "Trickster". She Knows All the Secrets of her mother and father. She Guards All the Riches of The SEA. She is The Wealthiest of all her family. She is held to be a Great Gossip. Those who represent her in dance, keep touching their fingers to their lips in the gesture of "Don't tell what I have said". When gossip is about, that no one can trace to its point of origin, it is said that *"Afrekete"* has started the rumor. On occasion those whom *"Afrekete"* possesses dance much like *"Legba"*.

"*Afrekete*" is much beloved by the "Dahomeans", who say she is the Most Powerful of her family.

The Children of "*SOGBO*" who Remained In The SKY, and who Control the Various Forms of "LIGHTNING" by means of which The "THUNDER PANTHEON" Punishes are:

"*ADEN*", born Next after "*AGBE*", and since "*Agbe*" no longer Lives In The SKY, "*Aden*" took the Rights of the Eldest Child. It is "*Aden*" who gives the Fine Rain which makes the Trees Bear Fruits. He is The Guardian of Fruit Trees. When He kills the man is found lying on his back.

"*AKOLOMBE*", Regulates The Temperature of The World. When it "Hails" he is responsible for it. He also causes Rivers to Overflow Their Banks. When he kills he takes away the lips of his victims.

"*AJAKATA*", gives the "Strong" Rain. Not the Rain which destroys but The Heavy Showers.
He always hurries, because he is the "Guardian of the Door to the Sky".

"*GBWESU*", remains with his mother "*SOGBO*", and His Voice is heard when Thunder mutters near

The Horizon. He does not come near earth, and never claims victims among men.

"AKELE", is another Thunder God that does not kill. It is said that he 'Holds The Cord of The Rain,' it being his duty to "Pull Up the Water From The SEA", out of which "The Rain" is made.

"ALASA", established himself in The SEA. *"Alasa"* went to *"Xevie"* to 'Teach Men The Nature of The Kingdom of The Earth and The Kingdom of The Sky.' He explained to the people of *"Xevie"* that the children of *"SOGBO"* were All *"SO"*, and taught the manner in which these *"SO"* should be worshipped, then he returned to The Sky. In consequence, it is the people of *"Xevie"* who were the First to address these *"SO"*.

When others learned of the worship of *"SO"* at *"Xevie"*, they came there to learn how to carry out the Rituals for *"SO"*. And thus the Religion of these GOD's in time spread everywhere. When *"Alasa"* returned to The Sky, he thought of *"Xevie"* on Earth, and remembering it with pleasure, he returned and settled there in a Great Forest, where he renders justice.

"GBADE", the Youngest Child of the "Thunder Pantheon", has all the freedom of The Earth and Sky, and though an evildoer, is never corrected. To him his

mother bequeath 'The Trait of Anger,' and since he is easily aroused, he wishes to annihilate all that he encounters.

He is the one who sends the "Jagged Lightning" that kills. His mother, who has a great weakness for him follows him about, and her gentle reproach is heard after the loud peals of Thunder, as she murmurs, "Do not kill. Do not kill. Calm yourself. Do not revenge yourself on mankind". His "Thunder" causes the Eggs of lizards, pythons and crocodiles to Open and thus their young are born. Since he is the strong and reckless one, when he kills, he strikes at all parts of the body.

"*SOGBO*" gave to him the Rainbow Serpent, "*AIDO HWEDO*", to transport him to Earth. As 'Executioner of Evildoers,' he comes more frequently than any of his brothers.

Thus it is when Clouds are seen from afar and A Murmur is heard, men know that "Rain" Falls even though they do not know where. It is then said that "*GBADE*" is visiting other countries. As the favorite of his mother, "*Gbade*" is as undisciplined and Powerful as is "*AFREKETE*" in The SEA Pantheon.

Religious Politics and the Myth of "ṢANGO"

by **Akinwumi Isola**
Professor, Department of African Languages & Literature,
Obafemi Awolowo University, Ile-Ife,
Osun State, Nigeria

Students of West African religion may claim to be familiar with The Myth of "*Sango*, the Yoruba God of Thunder". Having been popularized by many scholars, the details of the myth are usually Taken For Granted.

In **Hethersett's** account, in "Iwe Kika Ekerin Li Ede Yoruba" (Church Missionary Society, 1981) the most audacious 'Distortion' of the myth appears, either by Design or by Mistake. That the Distortion lasted for so long in Yoruba Society, reveals the disturbing tenacity of the Mental Enslavement to the Printed Word of the lettered elite. Once this Distortion appeared in print, it was taken as the Gospel Truth, and 'No One Bothered to Check Further Its Veracity,' from the illiterate Adherents of *Sango* Worship.

In this Investigation, we attempt to examine Hethersett's possible motives, if his Distortion was Deliberate. We also examine the possibilities of his making genuine Mistakes either through Ignorance or through indulging in folk ethnology. We finally present correct details of the *Sango* Myth, fruit of our current research.

Hethersett's Account:

According to Hethersett: *"Sango"* was the Fourth "Alaafin of Oyo", of tempestuous temper, and versed in the art of medicinal charms. In his attempt to eliminate at least one of his two restless war lords, Timi and Gbonka, causing instability in his domain, he set Timi to reign at "Ede", and sent Gbonka to challenge his authority, hoping that the encounter would lead to the death of at least one of them. Instead, however, Gbonka brought Timi back captive but alive. Alaafin ordered a rematch in his presence and openly supported Timi. Gbonka, the more powerful warrior, killed Timi and challenged the authority of *Sango.* In his violent reaction, *Sango* killed many of his own people and in his disappointment and frustration abdicated, and left the city of "Oyo", followed by many of his own people who nevertheless deserted him one by one until he was left only *Oya,* his favorite wife. When *Oya* also deserted him, he became utterly depressed and hanged himself. His close associates and friends planned a cover-up, because hanging oneself was and still is ignominious among the Yoruba. Anyone repeating the ugly story was seriously punished and soon everybody started saying "Oba Ko So" ("the king did not hang")."

This is "Hethersett's Account". Where Did He Get This Story? Before we examine the possibilities open to him, let us first discuss the problems with His Account.

To start with, he has some Historical Facts Wrong. (1) The episode of the Two Warlords "Timi" and "Gbonka" Did NOT Occur during the reign of The Fourth "Alaafin of Oyo". According to S. Johnson, ("The History of the Yoruba", 1901) it happened Much Earlier in the history of "OYO". Second, the name of "The Fourth Alaafin of Oyo" was NOT *"SANGO"*, according to C.L. Adeoye in *"Ase Ati Ise Yoruba"* 1979, He was called Babayemi Itiolu, who was versed in the art of Medicinal Charms.

It becomes clearer that Hethersett apparently just placed together a few facts Randomly Picked from Yoruba Mytho-history, to form this Potpourri presented as the Myth of *"Sango"*.

There is another misrepresentation: The Yoruba phrase *"OBA KOSO"*, the "King of *Koso*"; was translated *"Oba ko so"* (the "King did not hang"). This is a clear Distortion of the word *"Koso"*. *"KOSO"* was where the *"OBA SANGO"* Reigned, the Name of The PLACE. But if the word is broken into two separate syllables, the meaning changes: "Ko" means did not, "So" means hang. For a Mischievous Gospeller, the temptation to use this folk etymology might be too great to resist.

Hethersett was, by the way, 'the Headmaster of a Church Missionary Society School in Lagos, Nigeria.' Perhaps it was through the Deliberate Juggling of some facts of History and a folk etymological translation of *"Koso"*, that Hethersett derived His Myth of **Sango** according to the Church Missionary Society published in a "Yoruba Reader" meant for use in Their Christian Schools.

If this is the case, the Motives Appear Clear. The Early Forties was one of the Hottest Eras of 'Evangelization' in Yorubaland, and every avenue was pressed to Gain Converts.

Perhaps Hethersett's motives were to Popularize a Damaging Myth of *"SANGO"*, and thereby 'Discredit' one of the "Most Powerful and Feared Yoruba Deities".

"SANGO" is the Sworn Enemy of liars, thieves, and witches, and His Worship is Widespread indeed. Hethersett, a Headmaster and Evangelist, may have believed that the Popularization of a Degrading Myth about *"SANGO"* would do Enough 'Damage to His Image' to cause a Decline in adherence. If this is the case, he has succeeded by and large, but his success has been Restricted to the circle of the Educated Elite. The Real Adherents of *"SANGO"* Worship, largely illiterate (to Western languages), have been Unaware of the Existence of this Printed Distortion.

The Validity Test

There are Two Main Sources of Information about "Yoruba" Myth and History; the *"IFA"* Divination Poetry and the Large Body of *"Oriki"* (Praise Poetry) as contained in the Many "Oral" Genre.
Various verses of *"ESE IFA"* tell the story of *"SANGO"*. Some tell the story of his Deification, others document His Nature and Military Exploits.
One in particular, *"Ogbe-tura"*, recounts how *"Sango's"* presence came from *"ILE-IFE"* when *"OYO"* was founded.
Not a single verse in the whole *"IFA"* Corpus contain Anything Resembling Hethersett's Distortion.
'Any myth of a "Yoruba Deity" that cannot be found in *"ESE IFA"* Is Not Authentic.'
One important characteristic of Yoruba *"Oriki"* is that it tells the Whole Story of its subject, including all the unpleasant details.
That is why some scholars have preferred the translation "descriptive poetry", because *"Oriki"* is Not All Praise.
For example, in the "Onikoyi Lineage", the fact that their Progenitor was both a Warrior and a Thief constantly recurs. The "Okomi Linage" similarity "celebrates" the Promiscuity of their Female members.

No fact about a man Or a "Deity", however unpleasant, would be left out of The "*Oriki*".
It is therefore Significant to note that a Thorough Examination of the "*Oriki of SANGO*" reveals **NOTHING Suggesting "Suicide By Hanging".**

We can safely conclude that Hethersett's Account is NOT Accurate. Perhaps one of the reasons that the "Distortion" has existed for so long, is the 'Conspiracy of Silence.'
Apart from the fact that many people are Genuinely Ignorant of the Facts of the Myth, virtually everyone who could Read was either Christian or Moslem. It is possible that even if a Christian or Moslem had discovered the "Distortion", he might prefer to 'Leave It Uncorrected for the purpose of Religious Propaganda.'

The MYTH of *SANGO*

Early in 1983, I was interviewing a "Babalawo" (an "*IFA*" Priest), and as background to a question, I quickly retold "The Myth of *SANGO*" according to Hethersett.
The old man Stared at me, Concern written all over his face. He finally asked: "Learned one, where did you pick up that story?" When I told him that I read it in a

book, his surprise increased. He did not know that a "Book" could contain Lies.

I too was amazed to discover that what I read and believed for so long could be Untrue, and so began the search for the True Myth of *"SANGO"*.

The Babalawo took me through all the *"ODU"* that related to *"SANGO"* in the *"Ifa"* Divination Poetry. Among the important *"Odu"*: *"Otua-Oriko"* tells the story of <u>Sango's</u> Initiation Into the *"IFA"* Cult and the Origins of His Powers.

"Ofun-Eko" tells of Dancing as the main professions of *Sango*.

"Oworin-yeku" narrates how *"Sango"* seduced *"OYA"*, *"Ogun's"* Wife.

"Ika-Meji" documents many interesting episodes in *Sango's* life, and *"Ogbe-tura"* tells us how *Sango's* presence got to "OYO" from "ILE-IFE".

All these suggest that *"SANGO"* had existed at "ILE-IFE" long before the Founding of The City of "OYO". ****** Look Up *ODU's* ******

There is no space for us here to recite All the Verses that tell the stories of *"SANGO"* in all the *"Odu"* cited above. But it is important to our argument to relate the story in *"OGBE-TURA"*, which records how *"SANGO's"* Presence was transferred from "ILE-IFE" to "OYO", in order to reinforce our contention that (contrary to Hethersett's account) *"SANGO"* Could Not Have Been 'The Fourth "ALAAFIN of OYO".'

Summary of the Verse in "The Holy, *ODU IFA*
"OGBE-TURA"

It was the practice that every child of *"OLOFIN, OODUA"* old enough to choose a profession would be given the Tools necessary to establish himself in that trade. *"JEGBE"*, one of the children of *"OODUA"*, wanted to be a Hunter. His father gave him guns and gunpowder, and he went hunting. He killed a big Elephant and came home to announce it.
There was great joy, and people followed him into the forest to skin the animal. But the elephant had Disappeared miraculously. He killed other animals which also disappeared before anyone could come to see. People thought he was lying. Confused and depressed, he went to consult an *"IFA"* Priest.
The Priest asked him to make a sacrifice in the Forest. It was to be a burnt offering. The Fire he made at the site of the offering in the forest attracted a group of Kings who had gone to war but were lost in the forest.

When they found *"Jegbe"*, they asked him to lead them back to the city. *"Jegbe"* asked for his own share of their spoils of war and it was given. He led the group to the gates of *"Ile-Ife"*, where his father The *"Olofin, Oodua"* was King. He left the group at the gates and went alone to announce the arrival of the group of Kings. Because his story was strange and because of his reputation as a liar, no one believed him.

The *"Olofin, Oodua"*, told him he could keep whatever riches he had gotten, could lead the group he had discovered, and could be their King if he liked.

 "Jegbe" went back to the gates to lead the group into the city on horseback. Everyone was surprised! But *"Oodua"* had given *"Jegbe"* his word and was Honor-bound not to change his mind.

"Oodua" therefore asked *"Jegbe"* to lead the group to a New Site and be their "King".

 Since the group consisted of Kings, powerful men, *"Oodua"* gave *"Jegbe"* a "Conquering Sword" to deal with any revolts, and "THUNDERBOLTS", the Symbol of *"SANGO"*, to be his Guiding Deity. *"Jegbe"* led the group to found a new city, "OYO". That was how *"SANGO's"* Presence found its way to "OYO".

Since *"SANGO"* was there at the Foundation of "OYO" his Origin Could Not have been as the 'Fourth' "ALAAFIN of OYO".

"JEGBE" (*"ORANYAN"*), The First "ALAAFIN", established the Worship of *"SANGO"* (*"JAKUTA"*) and made it The State Religion with himself being The Chief, and *"SANGO"* Incarnate.

Who then was The Fourth "ALAAFIN of OYO", and why was it possible to confuse him with the Real *"SANGO"* of old?

The Important Tradition in "OYO" is to "Deify" each **"Alaafin"**. When on the Throne 'He Incarnates *"SANGO"*, and when Dead, He is "Deified" and Becomes *"SANGO"*.'

In that regard, every "ALAAFIN" is *"SANGO"*, so the 'Fourth' **"Alaafin"** Could be called *"SANGO"*. This practice brought the Proliferation of *"SANGO"* that we have today.

Apart from the fact that Each **"Alaafin"** was a *"SANGO"*, other Important men in history who were Devotees of *"SANGO"* started their own tradition of *"SANGO"* worship. And so today, we have Very Many *"SANGO"*, both in AFRICA and in The New World.

For example, we have *"SANGO OGODO"*, *"SANGO AGANJU"*, *"SANGO AFONJA"*, to mention only a Few.

But any of these traditions of *"SANGO"* worship Must NOT Be Confused with The Real Origin of *"SANGO"* which, according to the *"IFA ORACLE"* (the Main Source of Yoruba Religious Myths), existed in *"ILE-IFE"* even Before the City of "OYO" was founded.

Hethersett's Mistake seems therefore to have been that he Confused The 'Fourth' "ALAAFIN of OYO", himself a passionate Devotee of *"SANGO"*, with the Original *"SANGO"* in *"ILE-IFE"*, whose Symbols of Worship were brought along in Founding "OYO".

In spite of the Historical Inaccuracies in Hethersett's account, the life story he describes may have been Similar to that of "The Fourth, ALAAFIN of OYO". The fact remains, however, that the Real Story of *"SANGO"* is simply Not There.

■■■

Duro Ladipo's "Oba Ko So"

Duro Ladipo's folk opera "Oba Ko So" (The King Did Not Hang) is one of the most Popular in Yorubaland. The Opera, Actively Sponsored by the Institute of African Studies, of the University of Ibadan, was performed in Many of the world's cities.

The play was Based on 'Hethersett's Account', and the question has been often asked whether Duro Ladipo, like other young school boys, Fell Victim to the presumed authority of the written word and genuinely believed it to be Authentic. Later in life he Must Have discovered the Distortion, but perhaps thought it was Too Late to correct.
Other scholars believed that 'even if Duro Ladipo Had discovered the Distortion of Hethersett's account, he a Christian Son of an Anglican Catechist, might Not Have Bothered to Correct the Mistake. He remained a Christian merely Using The *"SANGO"* Myth for Profitable Entertainment.' Perhaps the truth is that once Ladipo Fell Victim to Hethersett's Distortion, he did not bother To Look Any Further.

Conclusion

Students of African Culture and African Religion in particular, **Must continue to Re-Examine Early Records that concern Traditional Religion, Especially those recorded during the time that Christian Evangelization was being Ruthlessly carried out.**
As we have seen, it is possible for researchers work to be Weakened either by His Own Religious Bias or simply by Ignorance.
Such Distorted Records may endure mainly because the illiterate but 'Knowledgeable Practitioners of African Religion cannot Read the Records in order to knock the bottom out of the Falsehoods.' The Lettered Elite that read the records, 'having been Taught to Trust Written Records, rarely venture Far Enough to question illiterate Practitioners.' **Only dedicated and dynamic questions Can Bring Such Distortions to Light.**

by **Akinwumi Isola**
……………………………………………………………………...

Samuel Johnson's 1846 - 1901"The History of the Yoruba", Published and Edited by: Dr. Obadiah Johnson in 1921, Lagos: C.M.S. Bookshops, Reprint 1966.   Samuel Johnson says;

"The ALAAFIN of OYO" were:
Oranmiyan (Oranyan)
Ajaka
Sango
Ajaka (reinstated)
Aganju
-------- Regent Iyayun
Kori
Oluaso
Onigbogi
Ofirin
Eguoju
Orompoto
Ajiboyede
Abipa
Obalokun
Ajagbo
Odarawu
Kanran
Jayin

Interregnum----------------------------
Ayibi
Osiyago
Ojigi
Gberu
Amuniwaiye
Onisile
Labisi
Awonbioju
Agboluaje
Majeogbe
Abiodun
Aole
Adebo
Maku
Interregnum------------------------------------ etc.

The ALAAFIN of OYO Empire

His Imperial Majesty

OBA LAMIDI OLAYIWOLA ADEYEMI III

(1970 -)

"The ALAAFIN of OYO"

The contest to his emergence began in 1968, when he was invited along with Ten others from his Ruling House to contest for the vacant stool of the "OYO" Empire.

As it was the custom of the land, there were three parameters with which the contestants were judged.

- First was eligibility,
- Second was popularity and
- Third, the stamina for the huge responsibilities of the office of The Alaafin of Oyo.

Oba Olayiwola Atanda Adeyemi emerged the first; defeating ten others after a vigorous screening exercise. However, due to what observer attested to be a political interference, the then government, "refused to endorse my appointment, saying the procedure was not right", were the words of this Great Monarch during one of the numerous interviews he granted. So the process started over again with the same result the second and the third time. Interestingly, despite the immense pressure upon **"The OYOMESI"**, against his candidature by the government, "The Oyomesi" stood its ground. Thus the process was put in abeyance until after the civil war, when the whole process started all over again.

To the relief of many, and chagrin of the opposition, Oba Adeyemi III was elected the winner and was finally chosen by **"The Oyomesi", The Kingmakers**, on November 18, 1970 and then moved into The Palace after completing the necessary Rites under the tutelage of "The Oyomesi".

In the process, he was inducted into the mysteries of various GODS like the *"IFA"* mysteries, and the *"SANGO"* mysteries. He was also made to undergo these inductions in order to be the Direct Representative of These Deities On Earth. He was taken through these processes so as to know all the chants, the proverbs, the oriki of all the past OBA's. More so, it was during the various purification and cleansing processes, at the hallowed grounds of Yoruba Ancient Shrines, that

Oba Adeyemi III made a "Covenant" with the illustrious Yoruba Ancestors, that he would defend, protect and add glamour to the Yoruba norms and Traditions; vowing to be the icon, the embodiment of Yoruba Culture, And, he had since then taken his Covenant seriously and had delivered the dividends of his covenant.

At an impressive Ceremony at the Durbar Stadium, OYO Town, Oba Adeyemi III was presented with the Staff of Office as "The ALAAFIN of OYO" in the presence of thousand of witnesses from all works of life and by the then Military Governor of the Western State, Colonel (retired General) Adeyinka Adebayo.

Then began the journey laden with a huge responsibility to protect, defend, project the cherished values of Yoruba customs and traditions with the zeal and if need be to lay down his life defending those values. Fortunately, and much to the relief of the Oyo Empire and the world, the need to lay down his life to defend Yoruba values never arose, hence his 70th birthday celebration, with 38 out of those years spent on the Throne of his forefathers.

The philosophy behind the "Alaafinate" as an institution is "duty for service and service to humanity". This translates that: once someone becomes The ALAAFIN, the totality of his life is 'Service to The People' and humanity in general. The Alaafin has no life of his own; day and night he is for the Service of the Yoruba Race, nay Humanity. In the cause of these many years, Oba Adeyemi III had striven to work strictly in accordance with the Oath he took in the presence of the "Oyomesi", on behalf of his people.

Being a self conscientious perfectionist, we make bold to say that he has worked assiduously and tirelessly with many governments both at the state and federal levels.

Beginning with General Adeyinka Adebayo (1971); Colonel Christopher Oluwole Rotimi, (1971-75); Navy Captain Akintunde Akinyoye, Aduwo, (August – September, 1975-83); Colonel David Mediaysese Jemibewon (1975-78); Colonel Paul Tarfa (1978-79); Chief Bola Ige the first elected governor, (1979-83); Dr. Victor Omololu Olunloyo second elected governor (October- December 1983); Colonel Oladayo Popoola, military governor (1984-85); Colonel Adetunji Idowu Olurin, military governor (1985-88); the late Colonel Sasaeniyan Oresanya, military governor (1988-90); late Colonel Abdulkareem Adisa, military governor (1990-92); Chief Kolapo Ishola, third elected governor

(1992-93); Naval Capitan Adetoye Sode, military administrator (1993-94); Colonolen Chinyere Ike Nwosu, military administrator (1994-96); Colonel Ahmed Usman, military administrator, (1996-98); Compol Amen Edore Oyakhire, military administrator (1998-99); Alhaji Lam Adeshina fourth elected governor (1999-2003); Senator Adewolu Ladoja (2003-2007); Otunba Adebayo Alao-Akala (the incumbent governor).

At the federal level, he has worked with General Yakubu Gowon, (1971-75); General Muritala Mohammed (1977-76); General Olusegun Obasanjo (1976-1979); Alhaji Shehu Shagari, the first executive president (1979-83); General Muhammed Buhari (1984-85); General Ibrahim Badamosi Babangida (1985-93); General Sani Abacha (1998-99); General Abdulsalami Abubakar Chief Olusegun Obasanjo (1999-2007); and president Umaru Yar'Adua.

During the agitation for the State creation in 1975, The Alaafin was first to fire the salvo, coupled with the efforts of others, the Old Oyo, Ogun and Old Ondo States were created. In recognition of his priceless and modest contributions to national development, he was invited as the only Oba from Yoruba land to perform the holy pilgrimage to Mecca with General Muritala

Muhammed. Other traditional rulers on the trip were the late Emir of Gwandu and the Otaru of Auchi, late Momodu Ikelebe II.

The Federal Government honoured this great achiever with the National Honour of CFR at the National Theatre, Iganmu, Lagos, in 1979.

In 1980, the Federal Government appointed "Kabiyesi, Oba Adeyemi" as the pioneering Chancellor of then newly established University of Sokoto, now Uthman Dan Fodio University, Sokoto, for a first four-year tenure.

At the expiration of that first tenure, the senate and council of the University recommended him for another term. The President and visitor to the University graciously approved the request, thus he was appointed for a second term. And at the expiration of the second term, in an unprecedented manner, has was appointed for yet another term, the third term, thus giving him a total of 12 years as the Chancellor of the University, a feat yet to be matched by anybody in the annals of Chancellorship of University of Nigeria.

It must be noted that for the period of those years, Oba Adeyemi III presented several academic and reasoned

memoranda on the university education and on contemporary issues published both Nationally and Internationally.
The University, in appreciation to his contributions and achievements, Honoured him with the Degree of Doctor of Letters (LL.D), Honoris Causa. At the time of Oba's Chancellor, the University recorded Absolute Peace as normal calendar was never disrupted for a day.

The monarch, in January 1988, installed Chief MKO Abiola as the Aare Ona Kankanfo in recognition of Abiola's contributions to the social, economic, cultural and political development of Yoruba land and Nigeria at large.

Two years later, the Federal Government under the administration of General Ibrahim Babangida, appointed The Alaafin as the Amiru Hajj operation to lead the Muslim faithful in the 21 states of the federation. The report of that year's Hajj operation remained the yardstick of measuring the success of Hajj operations in the country till date.

At his primary constituency as a Paramount foremost Traditional Ruler in Yoruba land, Oba Adeyemi III used his position to better the lots of many Obas, lifting many Non-crown wearing Obas to the status of Beaded

Crown wearers, not to mention his consistent fight for the improvement of their (the Obas') welfare at all times. These Obas spread through Oyo, Osun and Ogun. Some of those who benefited from this gesture were The Olubadan of Ibadan, Adebimpe, and The Soun of Ogbomoso, Oba Jimoh Oyewunmi Ajagungbade. "Following the powerful motion I moved at the floor of the Old Oyo State house of Chiefs, the government Approved the beaded crown of these two traditionals in 1976". The monarch said.

In 1975, The Onjo of Okeho got elevated. In 1977, The Onitede of Tede, Oba Olulokun too got the beaded crown. In 1979, The Aseyin of Iseyin, Oba Mashood Osuola, also got the beaded crown. Timi of Ede, the late Oba Oyelusi Tijani Agbaran II, also got elevated. In 1980 and 1981, The Oba of Kisi, Oba Yusuf Ariwajoye and The Okere of Saki, Oba Abimbola Oyedokun, and The Sabi Iganna got promoted respectively. Others were The Baale of Ile-Ogbo, who got elevated to the status of an Oba to Olu of Ile-Ogbo in 1995; Olubu of Ilobu, Oba Asiru Olatoye Olaniyan who got his own in 1986. The Alayegun of Ode-Omu, Akire of Ikire-Ile, Akirun of Ikirun, Aree of Ire, Olunisa of Inisha, all in Osun State also got beaded crown, courtesy of The Alaafin.

The Baale of Igboora, Jacob Oyerogba got elevated as a crown wearing Oba with the title of Olu of Igboora in 2001. In Ogun State, Oba of Ipokia got the beaded crown got elevated at the instance of the Alaafin. Last but not the least, Baale of Igangan, Lasisi-Aribiyan got elevated to the status of an Oba as Oba Lasisi Aribiyan, The Asigangan of Igangan and was awarded beaded crown in 2002. As a matter of fact, Oba Adeyemi III presented the crown to all of them at various towns with pump and pageantry.

In the exercise of his power as "The Chairman of the Council of Obas and Chiefs", in 1977 he caused meeting of The Council to be moved and be held in his Palace in OYO.

Childhood

Crown prince Lamidi Atanda Olayiwola Adeyemi's father, late **OBA (Alhaji) ADENIRAN ADEYEMI II**, being a staunch Muslim, mapped out his son's journey into education, starting from the Quranic School in Iseyin. He (Prince Lamidi) later went back to OYO but not into the Palace. Rather, he stayed with the head master at St. Andrews Primary School, (now St. Andrews College), proceeding thereafter to live with The Alake of Egba, Oba Oladepo Ademola, in his Palace.

Prince Atanda's education met a dead end following the 1947-48 demonstration of "Egba" women against "tax without representation" led by Mrs. Funmilayo Ransome Kuti. The effect forced Oba Ademola to abdicate his throne to live in exile at "Osogbo". That period was Prince Adeyemi's introduction into the other side of life he had never imagined to have existed. Mosquitos, home chores and lots more became his duty. But as they say, hardship only makes one tougher.

His father sent for him in 1948 and later sent him to live with Sir Kofoworola Adebayo Abayomi in Keffi, Ikoyi,

Lagos. While in Keffi, he attended Obalende Modern School, owned by Pa Domingo; father of the renowned musician Adeyomi Domingo. He later attended Tinubu Methodist School overlooking the famed fountain, the first General Bank.

Oba Adeyemi came second in his Entrance Examination into secondary schools in Lagos Island and was offered places at two great schools Igbobi College and St. Gregory's College, Obalende.
He chose to attend St. Gregory's College Obalende in accordance to his guardian's wish. Obalende was a cross-cultural settlement and living in there required wit and will, otherwise one will be walked over. Oba Adeyemi III lived in tough areas of Lagos Island. Places like Faji, Olowogbowo and the famed Ojuolomokoto.

His Sport Life

The ruler as many may have known and as many will find incredulous, is a sportsman. Before his ascension on to the throne of his forefathers, he trained and still trains as a boxer. He runs; jogs and plays football. Typically of him if time permits, he does as much as six kilometres and skips the rope.

His Growing Up

The Crown Prince Atanda Adeyemi could have grown in luxury and affluence as a Royal son should, but his growing was a far cry to what could have been. His father though not read appreciated the value of education through the contact he had with the British Administrative Officers that came to the Old Oyo Empire. Consequently, he lived to fight tooth and nail to see that his son was well read.

Needless to say, Oba Adeyemi III left St. Gregory's College with very good grades and had the choice to study Law, Economics or Public Relations. He chose to study Law because he majored in English doing both narrative and descriptive essays; coupled with a good retentive memory and a fantastic ability to remember dates and people, he felt his future in Law was secured.

Little did he know that fate had other plans in stock for him. His quest for Law changed when his father was deposed on February 14th, 1946 two days to the planned travel abroad.

He was offered a job at the Royal Exchange Assurance, Marina, Lagos. Despite the fact that he had landed where his dreams could not carry him, he made the best of every situation fate presented him. He wrote articles under pen names in newspapers, writing about himself and his experience.

One of his numerous articles was entitled **I SHALL BE GREAT** in 1968 and a year later, he wrote yet another one: **I Shall Be The Next Alaafin**. He wrote critiques of how the Nigerian teachers were treated, having been inspired by the state in which he saw one of his old teachers in a tattered shirt and tie.
He wrote yet another entitled. **Women Liberation: A Misnomer in Yoruba land**. This may not be unrelated to his view that women in the Oyo Empire were, in his words, "at least very active".

Shortly after his stay at the Royal Exchange Assurance, he was promoted into the 14th Floor into specialist area of obligatory Facultative Insurance and Internal memo drafting. He began to earn lots of money but his father gave a strict instruction that the must invest every penny that came his way.   Consequently, Oba Adeyemi III ventured into business buying wrecked cars to repair and resell.

Oba Adeyemi's journey had not been on a smooth path, rather he rode on the high stormy sea, sun-burnt mountains and many times on rock hilly parts. Having lost his mother, Ibironke, at an early age, he had little or No Motherly Touch and never had to stay for a long while with his father. He was almost always a lonely man. But his dreams and determination for success drove him heeding the Calls of The Gods, forgetting his own personal life for the sake of others, he has become an Icon, undoubtedly an **Iroko** tree: where all birds from the universe find their rest.

- Culled from the Maiden Edition of The **IMPERIAL MAGAZINE published October 2008.**

Thunder, Lightning and Storm Gods

ADAD
Assyro-Babylonian Myth

"ADAD" is usually represented standing on a "Bull" and grasping "Thunderbolts" in his hand. He is **"The God of Lightning and The Tempest"**. *"ADAD, The Tempest God"*, was also the God who brought the Beneficent "Wind" and with it the welcome "Rain". God of 'The Inundation Which Fertilizes,' who each year caused 'The River to Rise and Cover The Earth With Nourishing Slime.'

When *"BEL, Lord of The Land"* wished to send a series of plagues to chastise men he first addressed **"Adad"**. **"Adad"** served with *"SHAMASH, The Sun God"*, the privilege of 'Revealing The Future'. He was also the "Lord of Foresingt". His Companion was **"The Goddess, SHALA"**.

HADAD
Phoenician Myth

In "Ras Shamrah" texts **"BA'AL"** is **"HADAD, God of The Atmosphere, of Clouds and Tempest"**.

His Voice sounded in the Clouds, he wielded the "Thunderbolt", he dispensed "Rain". His Mother was *"ASHERAT-of-The-SEA"*. His Consort is **"The Goddess, ASHERAT"**. 'Lightning is **"BA'AL's** Earthly Saw.'

ZEUS
Greek Myth

Son of *"CRONUS and RHEA"*, was raised by the Two Nymphs *"ADRASTEIA and IDA"*. **"ZEUS"** began "The Age of the **Olympians**", before this the "**Titans**" ruled.
He was given the "Thunderbolt" by the *"Cyclopes"* in the war between the Titans and the Olympians (the New Gods).
From the Height of *"OLYMPUS"*, from the Height of "The Heaven", he hurled "Thunder and Lightning".
'With unwavering hand he flung bolts, and bolts, and the air was rent with sound and fury.' The fertile earth shuddered and burned.
Vast forests flamed and all things melted and boiled; the river, ocean, the immense sea and the entire earth.
Such was the mighty uproar of this Battle Among The GODS!

In spite of their pride and courage the "Titans" were finally defeated. He also warred against the "Giants" who attacked *"Olympus"*. And together with the "Olympians" and "Heracles" (Hercules=Roman) they defeated the "Giants".
He also defeated *"Typhoeus"*, sent by *"GAEA"*, with his Thunderbolts.
The defeat of *"Typhoeus"* assured the final lasting Supremacy of ***"ZEUS"*, uncontested "Master of Gods and Man"**.
The most famous Sanctuary of **"ZEUS"** was that of "Dodona", in "Epirus". His attributes are the "Scepter" in his left hand, in right hand the "Thunderbolt" and his feet the "Eagle". Often he wears a "Crown of Oak-leaves".

JUPITER
Roman Myth

The **"Etruscan" JUPITER**, who was called "TINIA", function was to 'warn men and to punish them.' For this purpose he possessed Three **"Thunderbolts"**.
He could hurl the first whenever he liked, as a Warning. To hurl the Second as a warning, he had to get permission of Twelve Gods. The Third "Thunderbolt"

was the one which Punished. It could only be released with the consent of Superior or Hidden Gods.

This Primitive *"JUPITER"* ("Daylight Thunder") can be compared with *"SUMMANUS"* ("Nocturnal Thunder") another "Etruscan Thundergod".

The **"Latin" JUPITER** was first of all **"The God of Light"**—"Sun and Moon"—and of Celestial Phenomena; "Wind, Rain, Thunder, and Lightning".

"JUPITER" became the Great Protector of the City and the State. He was a "Warrior-God". He symbolized the great virtues of justice, good faith and honor; and protector of youth.

Worshipped throughout "Italy", a very ancient Temple for *"JUPITER"* was the "capitolium vetus". Here he formed a Triad with *"JUNO"* and *"MINERVA"*.

DONAR – THOR
Teutonic Myth

"THOR, The God of Thunder", whose name in old "German" was *"DONAR"* has been revered by all the "Teutonic" Tribes. Some considered him as the 'First and the Most Powerful of all The GODS.'

Roman authors often identified him with "Jupiter".

The "Germans" named Thursday after *"Donar"* or *"Thor"*, Donnerstag (German) Thursday (English). He was a much Feared Divinity. When the "Thunder" Rolled people believed they heard 'The Wheels of *"DONAR's"* Chariot on the vault of Heaven.' When the "Thunderbolt" Struck they said the God had 'Cast His Fiery Weapon from On High.' This Weapon was represented as a "Missile Axe", or Stone "Hammer", *"THOR's"* habitual Attribute. The "Germans" invoked *"DONAR"* and Chanted His Glory when marching into battle.

In certain northern countries, particularly in "Norway", *"THOR"*- the German *"Donar"*- finally prevailed over all the Other God's. Norse poets saw him as the very apotheosis of the "Warrior", rude, simple, and noble, always ready to face combat and danger, a tireless adversary of Giants and Demons, a Hero without fear, who disdained repose.

PYERUN
Slavonic Myth

"PYERUN", was "God of War" according to old "Russian" chronicles, and the Pagans considered the "Thunderbolt" the Most Divine Weapon.
He is "The GOD Who Wields the Thunderbolt" and they recognize him as The Sole "Lord of the Universe". At "Kiev" the idol of *"PYERUN"* was erected on a Hill, under the open Sky, and the functions of The Priests were performed by The "Kniaz", or Prince Military Chieftain of the city.

UKKO
Finno – Ugric Myth

"UKKO, The God of Thunder", was 'The Ancient Father Who Reigns in The Heavens.'
He was "The God of The Sky and Air". It was he who supported The World, who gathered The Clouds and made The Rain fall. He was invoked only when all the other Gods had been called in vain.
"UKKO's" weapon was a "Hammer, Axe or Sword", by which he Struck "Lightning". While *"UKKO"* mated with his wife *"AKKA"*, there was a "Thunderstorm".

He Created "Thunderstorms" also by 'Driving with His Chariot in the Clouds.' The original Weapon of *"UKKO"* was probably the 'Boat-shaped Stone Axe', The *"VASARA", "UKKO's Hammer"*.

Cults of Fire, Lightning and Storm

Ancient Persian Myth

The **"Mazdaians"** were called "ateshperest" or "FIRE"-worshippers.

In the Traditionalist organization of *"The MAGI"*, the "Fire Chiefs", occupied an Eminent Position.

The Myth of **"ATAR"**, "Fire", is only an Expression of this Cult. **"The Element of FIRE"**, personified, he brings men comfort, grants them the wherewithal to live, wisdom, virility, noble offspring and paradise.

He defends The World against the enterprise of the Evil One.

Before their conversion to "Islam", The ARABS practiced a Naturalistic and Animistic Religion. They peopled the Universe with *Demons,* the *"JINNS"*, and with redoubtable *Genii,* the *"EFRIT"*, who delighted in assuming the most diverse forms in order to harm or help mankind. Their Gods and Goddesses numbered in the Fifties, and Their **"God of Storm and Tempest"** was **"KUZAR"**.

INDRA
The Kshatriyas

The **"Kshatriyas"**, the Warrior Nobility, the **"Aryans"** who set yokes on the people of the dark race, worshipped in **"INDRA"** the grandiose projection of his own type. He is armed with Arrows and rides a Chariot, like a Nobleman.

The myth transforms him into a Cosmic Force, and he wields a "Thunderbolt", The "Lightning", while his Chariot Becomes "The Sun".

"INDRA" cleaves Demons asunder, The Swashbuckler who swills 'Ambrosia', not to Live but to Get Drunk.

He is the only one of the *"VEDIC" GODS* who appears *Human* in his Characteristics and his Morals, and to him is addressed by far the largest number of Hymns.

As he supplies both "Light" and "Water" he appears not only as **"The GOD of War"** but as the **"Principal of Fertility"**.

He Reigns in The Sky and Triumphs in The Storm, when he *"Thunders"* and lets loose The *"Rains.*

AGNI
The Brahman

The **"Brahman"**, the Priestly Caste, **"AGNI"** is the Personification of **"FIRE"**. It started as the Instrument of The Cult, and became The Object. The same "Flame" waves and crackles on the Hearth in the burning sunshine, and in the Flash of "Lightning".

So **"AGNI"** like *"INDRA"*, but in another sense, became the equivalent of the *'Starry Hearth-fire of The World, and of the "Lightning" which hurls down "Rain" on the thirsty earth.'*

He is described as a Red man with Three Legs, Seven Arms and black eyes and hair. He rides on a "RAM", and wears the **"Brahmanic Cord"** with a Garland of Fruits. "Flames" spout from his mouth, and his body sends forth "Rays of Light".

His attributes are "The Axe", wood, the bellows (a fan), the torch and the "Sacrificial Spoon".

He is called **"The Son of Heaven and Earth"**, The Son of *"BRAHMA"*.

He made "The Sun, and *filled the night with Stars.*" 'The Gods Fear Him and Do Homage To Him, for He Knows the Secrets of Mortals.'

LEI-KUNG
Chinese Myth

"Taoist" Religion includes a whole "Ministry of Thunder" made up of Several Divinities.
The people recognize only One *"THUNDER GOD"* called **"My Lord Thunder, LEI-KUNG"**.
By Order of Heaven, "The Thunder" Punishes Human Beings Guilty of Great Crime which has remained undetected or which human laws do not touch; it also punishes "Evil Spirits" who by practicing "Tao Doctrine", have succeeded in Gaining Personality and make use of it to Harm mankind, etc.
During Storms, *"THUNDER"* is helped by Several Other Divinities;
Flashes of LIGHTNING, **"TIEN-Mu"**,
RAIN, **"YU-Tzu"**, CLOUD, **"YUN-T'ung,**
WIND **"Feng-Po"** or **"Feng-P'o-P'o.**

SUSANOO
Japanese Myth

"SUSANOO" was a "Fertility God", closely linked with Agricultural beliefs. At one and the same time He is a **"God of Thunder, Storm and Rain"**. He is associated with "Snakes", for in Ancient "Japan" the *"Snake"* was considered as *"The God of Thunder"*. The main Descendants of **"The God, SUSANOO"** are related either to "Water", "Thunder", or "The Snake". Many of his exploits are written in the Stories of the *"Kojiki"* and *"Nihon Shoki"*.

TAKE-MIKAZUCHI

"TAKE-MIKAZUCHI" is also considered a **"God of Thunder"**. His Son **"Ajisuki-Takahikone"** is also considered a **"Thunder God"**. At his birth he cried and screamed so much, to calm him they carried him to the top and the bottom of a "Ladder".
In the "Japanese" mind **"The Ladder"** is used to 'get to Heaven,' the characteristic of the **"Thunder"** is to 'come and go to Heaven and Earth.' He was also placed in a "Boat". The **"Boat"** was means by which *"The Thundergod Connected Heaven and Earth"*.

"KAMI-NARI, The God of Rolling Thunder", is also Greatly Venerated, many Sanctuaries are devoted to him.

HINO
Iroquois Myth

One of the Most Important among The Chief God's of the **"Iroquois"** is **"HINO, The Thunder Spirit"**. He is **"Guardian of The Sky"**. Armed with a Powerful "Bow and Arrows of **FIRE**", he destroys all harmful things. His Wife is **"The Rainbow"**.

THUNDER BIRD
Algonquin Myth

The **"Algonquin"** Nation believe in **"The THUNDERBIRD"**, a Powerful Spirit whose Eyes Flash **"Lightning",** while the Beating of his Wings is the Rolling of **"Thunder"**.
'He prevents the Earth from Drying Up and Vegetation from Dying.'
He is escorted by "Spirits" who are represented in the form of Birds resembling "Falcons" or "Eagles".
Most of the "Plains Indians" believe in **"The Thunderbird"**. To them, "THUNDER" is the **"Voice of The Great Spirit"** Speaking in The Clouds.

TIRAWA
Pawnee Myth

The **"Pawnee"**, believed that before **"The Great Chief, TIRAWA"**, before Creating Man, sent **"Lightning"** to 'explore The Earth with a Sack of Storms' in which he had enclosed *The Constellations,* which he hung in The Sky.

BIG HAWK
THUNDERBIRD CLAN – FIRE
Chippewa Myth

Once there was a **"BIG HAWK"**, the Biggest "Hawk" that had ever lived on The Earth. Luckily for the people this "Hawk" was Good and Kindly toward all those who were around him. Besides being Big, this "Hawk" was also Very Powerful. He could sing a Special Song and all of the Hawks from all over the territory would come to counsel with him. He could Sing another that would catch "Rain Clouds" that were in the vicinity and bring them toward him. He was a Very Powerful Hawk.

This **"Hawk"** was so Powerful that The **"THUNDER BEINGS"** one time decided to 'give him a **Special Song**' that he could sing that would Draw Them to him. They told him that to 'Sing That Song Correctly' he First had to build a Circular Lodge large enough for Himself and all of the Other Animals he wanted to invite. He had to make a Circular Alter of a Special Kind and put particular things from the Mineral, the Plant and the Animal Kingdom on it.

He had to 'Give Thanks to the **"GREAT SPIRIT"** Before he sang this song,' and that he had to Feel Gratitude to **"The Thunderers"** for Sharing Their Power with him.

One summer he decided to sing this Song, so he did as the **"Thunderers"** had told him. He invited some Hawks and some of the Other Birds to come into the Lodge with him. They accepted, and when the song was done and **"The Thunderers"** had come, they all left the Lodge knowing that they had been given Special Powers from having heard the song.

"BIG HAWK" had gathered *Remarkable Powers* to him, and now A Touch of His Wings could "Heal" his friends from even the gravest wounds. All of the "Power" that he had became Too Much for **"Big Hawk",** and instead of 'Remembering to Give Thanks Every Morning to The **"Great Spirit",**' he began to get

Huffed Up and to go around singing, "I Am the Most Powerful Hawk of Them All. I Am Great….Kaik Kaik Kaik."

"The **GREAT SPIRIT**" looked at the **Hawk** and was Patient, hoping that he would remember. But He Did Not. He just got more and more Huffed Up.

The next summer he decided that, once again, he would Sing the Song of **"The Thunder Beings"** so he could get even More Power. He decided that he was *So Powerful* he Did Not have to bother building "The Lodge" or 'Make the Preparations he had been told to make.' He didn't even bother to 'Give Thanks to **"The Great Spirit"** or to The **"Thunderers".**' He invited all the birds and animals who would come to Witness His Power.

He began to Sing His Song 'just sitting in his Nest in the biggest tree around,' and he Preened Himself and Huffed Himself Up More as **"The Thunderers"** approached.

Suddenly, a Bolt of **"Lightning"** Shot Out from one of the Clouds, and 'Burst into Balls of Flame' just as it touched the Tip of **Big Hawk's** Wing. Just as suddenly, 'the Ball of Flame and the **Hawk** Disappeared' before any of the other animals were hurt. They all looked around, not believing their eyes.

"Big Hawk" found himself up in The Sky talking with the **"Great Spirit"**.

"Big Hawk", said **"The GREAT SPIRIT"**, "You have become Too Arrogant. You Forget to Give Your Thanks. You Forget the Rituals and Ceremonies that you have been given. You Forget the Real Source of Your Power. Since you have Insulted the **"Thunder Beings"** by misusing The Gift that they gave to you, you will now become Their Servant. You will still be a big handsome bird, but 'You Will No Longer Be Able to Call The **"Thunder".'** Now They Will Call You. Whenever **"The Thunderers"** go out to do their work, you will be with them. So you don't get too Huffed Up from people seeing you, you will always be Hidden Partly behind the Clouds. You will appear to some as a strange 'Cloud Formation.' You will appear to others as a 'Fiery Shape' created by the **"Lightning"**. Only those with Very Clear Sight will see you as you are, as the **"BIRD of FIRE, The THUNDERBIRD"**.
Go Now, and serve until you learn the pleasure that can come from Serving, and from Remembering Your Place In The Universe."

And so **"The Thunderbird"** came to the people. **"Thunderbird Clan"** Folk will always want to place themselves in an area where they get Good Sun at least part of the time and where the "Thunder and Lightning" sometimes come to call to them. They seem to Need 'the Energy of "Natural Fire" in all of its many forms to Strengthen and Renew the **Fire** that Always Burns Within Them.' **ASE! ASE! ASE!**

TLALOC
Aztec Myth

In accordance with the custom of Conquering Pagans, the **"Aztecs"** felt they ought to Revere The God's of the conquered. Thus New Cults grew up.
Several of their **Great Gods** had such an origin, particularly **"QUETZALCOATL"** who was of **"Toltec"** Origin and **"TLALOC"** an Ancient Deity of the **"Otomi"**.
"TLALOC" ("pulp of the earth") was **"The God of Mountains, Rain, and Springs"**. He is painted Black, but wears a Garland of White Feathers topped with a Green Plume. Among his attributes is the Mask of the Two-headed Snake.
"Tlaloc" lived on the Mountain Tops, and his dwelling "Tlalocan" was abundantly provided with food. There lived **"The GODDESSES of Cereals, and Maize"**.
 "Tlaloc" owned "Four Pitchers of **Water**" which he used for watering The Earth. The Water of the First was Good, and helped the growing of maize and fruits; that of the Second produced Spiders' Webs and caused

blight among the cereals; that of the Third turned to Frost, and that of the Fourth Destroyed all fruits.

For his Festival, numerous Children and Babies at the breast were Sacrificed to Him. If the children cried and shed plenty of tears the spectators rejoiced, saying that Rain was coming.

"CHALCHIUHTLICUE, Goddess of Running Water, Springs and Streams", was his wife or sister. She was invoked 'For the Protection of New-born Children, marriages, and chaste loves.'

HURAKAN
Maya Myth

In "Guatemala" there exists a Powerful God called **"HURAKAN"** known also in the "West Indies". He presides over **"The Whirlwind"** and the Rumbling of the **"Thunderstorm".** He gave the **"Maya"** "Fire" by rubbing his Sandals together. His surname is **"TOHIL"**, a name given **"The Great God, QUETZALCOATL, of The Aztec"**

CATEQUIL
Inca Myth

The **"Inca"** had a Deity called "CATEQUIL, The THUNDER and LIGHTNING GOD", represented carrying a "Sling and a Mace". Children were Sacrificed to him, and "Twins" were looked upon as his children.

PILLAN
Araucanians – Chile

The **"Araucanians"** of "Chile" have a Chief God, **"PILLAN, The God of Thunder"**, who was also **"The God of Fire"**. He caused Earthquakes, Volcanic Eruptions, and Lightning.

They represented him as a 'Corporeal Deity having several forms at once.' The Chiefs and Warriors killed during a war were absorbed into **"Pillan"**, the former became "Volcanoes", the latter became "Clouds".

TUPAN
Tupinambas – Brazil

The **"Tupinambas"** of "Brazil" had a Very Important Power of **"Thunder and Lightning"** called **"TUPAN"**. He used a "Boat" to Cross The Sky. Each journey caused a Storm, and the noise of **"Thunder"** comes from the Hollow Seat he used in the Boat.

Two attendant "Birds" take their place in his "Canoe", and are considered by the "Tupinambas" as Heralds of Storms, which only stop when **"Tupan"** has reached his Mother.

ŞANGO PIPE

(ORIKI ŞANGO)

Owner of knowledge, brilliant eye
He splits the Sky open absolutely
He kills the person who oversteps authority,
and closes his door
Powerful return, for whom we pound the mortar
He rides and returns on the head of the Axe
Like Trickster, he stands; one knee bent
the other straight
He dances precisely, while gazing at the Sky

HAIL *"SANGO"*!!!!

Man with a solid build
He listens to the man who brings him offerings,
He leaves in confusion the contentious man
Wizard of the Sky
He enters the Palace balancing 800 large sacks
upon his head
Leopard with Flaming Eyes
Storm on the edge of a knife
He dances savagely in the courtyard of the Impertinent

Victorious Shere
Orobondo Oshe

AFONJA, carrying Fire as a burden on his head
Small Bird, Exceeding Force
If someone exercises his Penis, he provokes jealousy,
unlike the child who has never had sex,
unlike the elder who is finished with sex
Son of Akani, against the unforeseen,
let us do things together

His very glance supports his followers
He dances in a martial manner,
Stalwart, like Oshe

Fire mounts the roof of the place of The King
Crown Becomes Two
Anyone who waits for the elephant waits for death!
Anyone who waits for the buffalo waits for death!

SANGO who rides Fire like a horse
Draped in a cloth of death
SANGO who strikes the one who is stupid
SANGO who wrinkles his nose and the liar
runs away
You think the worm is dancing,

but that is merely the way he walks,
You think *SANGO* is fighting you,
but that is merely the way he is
SANGO walks alone, but he enters the town
like a swarm of locusts

He is cool when he kills, cool when he eats
You look in haste, you die in haste
We do not know how bees make honey,
SANGO-is-always cool
We do not know how porcupine stands his quills on
end,
SANGO-is-always-cool
We do not know how Ajomagbodo makes fitting
Heaven above

OBA KOSO!!!!

Onibante owo jigbede
Owner-of-the-vest-of-glittering-coin

Alado lube yombala
Man-who-splits-the-mortar-resonantly

Areku jaiye
One-who-wears-the-cloth-of-death-while-
still-alive

SANGO Okunrin meje
SANGO-seven-men-in-one

Onimonsimo, eke nsa
Onimonsimo-causing-the-liar-to-run-away

Asingbere Ogun leyinju
Asingbere-ogun-at-the-back-of-the-eyes

Aira Oluwa mi ko so
My-lord-Aira-did-not-hang

Akin Oba Osha
Brave-King-Osha

Ayi wo Kabiyesi
Don't-stare-at-the-King

Ekun oloju ina
Leopard-owner-of-the-eyes-of-fire

Ewe gbe mi awala-wulu omo A-gb'-Egun ko fo,
Lubayemi, omo A fi igba ata se-'gun,
Afin'ju el'ewa ru-'l'-ekun Orun gbongan-gbongan
Leaves help me mumble-mumble the child-of-one-who-
conquers-with-two-hundred-peppers,
Beautiful neat person-opens-the-door-of-the-Sky-
so-it-sounds-gbongan-gbongan

HAIL *"SANGO"*!!!!

OLUFIRAN OBA KOSO
OBA ASANGIRI
ALAGIRI
OLAGIRI KA KA KA KOMO KUNRIN KO

SANGO!!!!
EKURU GBAGBA L'ODA
ILE GBOGBO, AKURO L'OFO

ENIA TI A BU LEHIN, T'O SI MO
ENIA TI A BU LEHIN, T'O SI GBO
OGUNLABI!
ETI LU KA 'RA BI AJERE

MA BU U
MA SA A
MA S'ORO RE LEHIN
BABA BAMKOLE!

SANGO O!!!!
ORU-OWO-R' OWU
ORU FEE-FEE-RE 'FE
ORU-GUDUBU-TA-N' GUDUBU

SANGO O!!!!
DEGOKE!!!!
AREMU!!!!

HAIL *SANGO!!!!*
OLUFIRAN, THE KING DID NOT HANG
THE KING WHO CRACKS THE WALL
HE WHO SPLITS THE WALL
HE WO SPLITS THE WALL HERE AND THERE
AND CURLS UP THE YOUNG MAN

SANGO!!!!
DUST, DUST, AND DUST AGAIN IN THE DRY
SEASON
EVERY INCH OF GROUND LIKE MARSHY FARM
SOIL IN THE WET SEASON

A MAN WHO GETS TO KNOW WHO HAS
SPOKEN ILL OF HIM BEHIND HIS BACK
A MAN WHO HEARS ALL THAT IS SAID OF HIM
BEHIND HIS BACK
OGUNLABI!
THERE ARE EARS ALL OVER HIS BODY LIKE
HOLES IN A COLLANDER

DON'T ABUSE HIM
DON'T HACK HIM
DON'T BACK BITE HIM
BABA BAMKOLE!

SANGO O!!!!
THE MAN WHO CARRIED RAW COTTON
TO OWU
THE MAN WHO CARRIED YAM FLOUR
TO IFE
THE MAN WHO CARRIED GUDUBU YAMS TO
GUDUBU TOWN

SANGO!!!!
DEGOKE!
AREMU!

Oriki OYO

Bi etu ba wo ile
jejene ni mu ewure
Bi SANGO ba wo ile
jejene ni mu osa gbogbo

A ri ru ala oninanso
Gangan ni ile ni igbo soro ibosi
A ji kun osun bi oge
Eniru oko Lamutata
O gbe ile suru gbe omo si
Oko Ibeji

Oriki OUIDAH

Olubisi eranko yayo agan obinrin
Tapa ma fi ogo yonu
Tapa ma fi odi ogo tele fo magamaga

O ku Tapa osoro sin
Awe Tapa osoro gba
Ni ojo Tapa ba ku own ni o wa faran oyin wa
Faran Oyin dowan
Faran owu dopo
Ayi peri aja kaja ki o ku
Ayi peri agbokagbo ki a re orun

Oriki KETOU

SANGO jigi li oko
A to fi se ogun ran
Kerekele a bi erukun gbongbo
Ajanan bebebe ti nru odo eru wo ilu
A ja ewu odan sa li ogun
Ewon ja nibo o wu
Ebiti fi owo ponhin soro
Alamula ekun, oko Orisa aniyan ina

A ke aso leri oku bo Iyawo
O kan okuta ni igbo ki o se eje
A ru okuta ma se osuka

Ekun oko OYA
Jo OSANYIN
Oni ile esin
Oni ibon asosoyi
Oko kangiri sehin

Prayer *ADJA-WERE*

Bara ki awa ji ire
Li awa ji e ki
O ji ero ma ri ese
Eri oku ko jinna
Ajidigbi bi ina rin
ki awa ji ire
Ona Mogba ki awa ji ire
Otun Mogba ki awa ji ire
Osi Mogba ki awa ji ire
Ekerin Mogba ki awa ji ire
Mogba aiye
Mogba Orun

Sere Ajase
Baba wa ojo
Ose Ogbondo
Ejila esebora
Oba gbo
Oba de
Oba jigi

References

Akinwumi Isola;
"Religious Politics and The Myth of Sango".
"African Traditional Religions In Contemporary Society": Edited by Jacob K. Olupona.

A. Isola;
"Sango Pipe - One Form of Yoruba Oral Poetry". M.A. Thesis, University of Lagos 1971

Gary Edwards and John Mason;
"Black Gods Orisa Studies In The New World". Yoruba Theological Archministry, Brooklyn, NY 1985

Oba Ofuntola Oseijeman Adelabu Adefunmi I;
"Olorisha – A Guidebook Into Yoruba Religion", Great Benin Books 1982

Rev. Samuel Johnson;
"The History of The Yoruba" (1897).
Edited by, Dr. O. Johnson, Published 1921, London. Reprinted in 1970 by Negro Universities Press, Westport Conn. USA J.

J. Lorand Matory;
"Sex and The Empire That Is No More", Berghahn
Books 2005. ["SANGO Initiation", Igboho, 1988]

Babatunde Lawal;
"Yoruba Sango Sculpture In Historical Retrospect",
Ann Arbor University Microfilms, 1970

William Bascom;
"The Yoruba of Southwestern Nigeria", Holt, Rinehard
and Winston, N.Y. 1969
"Sango in the New World", African and African
American Research Institute, Austin 1972

Melville J. Herskovits;
"Dahomey, An Ancient West African Kingdom",
Northwestern University Press, Evanston 1967

Robert Farris Thompson;
"African Art In Motion", University of California, Los
Angeles 1974
R.F. Thompson; "Flash of The Spirit", Vintage Books
1983

Bernard Maupoli;
"La Geomancie a L'Ancienne Cote Des Enclaves" –
Translated by H.L. Medahochi Kofi Zannu,
"Holy Lessons from The Sacred Odu of IFA",
Milwaukee, USA

J.F.Ade Ajayi & Michael Crowder;
"History of West Africa", Columbia University Press,
N.Y. 1976

"Larousse Encyclopedia of Mythology", Prometheus
Press, New York 1959

C.L. Adoye; "Asa Ati Ise Yoruba",
Oxford University Press. Ibadan 1971

Chief O.A. Fagbenro Beyioku;
"Ifa Its Worship and Prayers", Salako Press EB Nigeria

"Oshogbo Celebrates The Festival of SANGO", Nigeria
Magazine 1953

Sun Bear & Wabun Bear;
"Medicine Wheel-Earth Astrology", Prentice Hall Press
N.Y. 1980

About The Author

Iya Afin, Ayobunmi Sosi Sangode is a Senior Priestess of *"SANGO*, The Deity of Thunder and Lightning". She was the Chief Priestess of *"SANGO"* (1978-1980's) at the Temple of *"SANGO"* in Oyotunji African Village, where she resided with her husband The Oluwo *IFA* of Oyotunji, and Minister of Foreign Affairs, the late H.L. Chief Adenibi Edubi Ifamunyiwa Ajamu.

H.L. Iya Sangode is the "Iya Alaase *SANGO*" of the "*SANGO*" Temple at Oyotunji. She is the Published Author of:
"The CULT OF SANGO" : The Study of Fire;
"RITES OF PASSAGE / Psychology of Female Power";
"The GODDESSES / Psychology of Female Power", Part II;
"The SISTERHOOD / Psychology of Female Power" Part III.
She is the Artist "SOSI" whose Spiritual and Traditional African Art can be seen in many homes and Shrines from Florida to Calif., and also in the Traditional "African Village of OYOTUNJI" in the Sea Islands of So. Carolina.
As a Initiated Priestess in her Culture (May 1974), she has been a Teacher and Trainer of Priests, with a Masters and PhD in Para-Psychology & Theological Studies from the "African Theological Archministry" (ATA), and spends her time Writing and Lecturing on Women's Spirituality, Rites of Passage and Women's Studies.

CPSIA information can be obtained
at www.ICGtesting.com
Printed in the USA
LVHW081541170621
690493LV00019B/943

9 781502 719829